Scats
and
Tracks

of the
Desert Southwest

A Field Guide to the Signs of 70 Wildlife Species

James C. Halfpenny, Ph.D.

Illustrated by Todd Telander

FALCON®

GUILFORD, CONNECTICUT
HELENA, MONTANA

AN IMPRINT OF THE GLOBE PEQUOT PRESS

CAUTION

Outdoor recreational activities are by their very nature potentially
hazardous. All participants in such activities must assume responsi-
bility for their own actions and safety. The information contained in
this guidebook cannot replace sound judgment and good decision-
making skills, which help reduce exposure, nor does the scope of this
book allow for the disclosure of all the potential hazards and risks
involved in such activities.

Learn as much as possible about the outdoor recreational activities in which you participate, prepare for the unexpected, and be cau-
tious. The reward will be a safer and more enjoyable experience.

To Diann, my alpha partner,
ursophile, and tracking friend, for
all her loving support and help.

Acknowledgments

First and foremost, I wish to thank all my students for their years of questions and help, but most of all for the time we've shared tracking and studying in the field. I also wish to thank Don Clark, Deborah Cowman, Lee Fitzhugh, Murie Museum, Lance Peck, Phil Yanimoto, and Teton Science School.

Contents

Introduction

In the late 1970s, the era of "watchable wildlife" arrived in the United States. Baby boomers wanted to turn to and experience the outdoors. Television brought wildlife closer than ever. Bird watching thrived. Now more than ever, millions of people want to watch wild animals. Wildlife are not always easy to find and observe, though. Finding their tracks and signs is an exciting alternative to actually seeing the animals. "Trackable wildlife" adds another dimension to the outdoor experience. Todd and I wish to share that dimension, the joy of reading stories written in the soil and snow.

Upwards of ten books on tracking have been written in the United States during each decade of the 20th century. Most are general, covering the United States or all of North America. In *Scats and Tracks of the Desert Southwest*, we focus on one biogeographic region, with details about the region's most common or characteristic species of mammals, birds, reptiles, and amphibians. (We have included a few rare species because of their particular interest or significance in a region. For example, what a coup it would be to document a jaguar in Arizona.) We've intentionally limited the number of species covered in order to keep the information manageable. This guide is small, allowing you to carry it in a pack or pocket and use it frequently.

As your knowledge and interest in tracking grows, you may want to find additional information and help. Key references are listed in Selected Reading. For a more detailed investigation of tracking, I recommend my book *A Field Guide to Mammal Tracking in North America* (1986, Johnson Publishing, Boulder, CO), and titles by Olaus Murie, L. R. Forrest, and Paul Rezendes.

One organization will, in computer parlance, provide interactive access to expand your tracking background. A

Naturalist's World (ANW) is an ecologically oriented company dedicated to providing educational programs and materials reflecting the natural history of North America. Diann Thompson and I run the daily business, teach classes, and lead programs. Our on-site classes provide hands-on experience and in-depth information about animals, their tracks, and the ecology of their environments. In addition to tracking classes, our field programs cover bears, wolves, winter ecology, the northern lights, and alpine ecology. ANW also provides books, videos, slides shows, and computer programs for self-study and as teaching and field aids. You can check out ANW on the internet at www.tracknature.com.

Class schedules, product information, and information about ANW can be obtained from P.O. Box 989, Gardiner, Montana 59030, phone (406) 848-9458, or on the world-wide web at www.tracknature.com.

Keep on tracking!

—*James C. Halfpenny*

About tracking

Tracking is for everyone, beginner and expert, young and old. The fun of nature's challenge is solving the mystery written in the trail. Prepare yourself by learning the backgrounds and basics of tracking before exercising your skills in the field.

Field notes and preserving tracks

To the natural history detective, the track and trail are things of great beauty and significance. They tell part of the story of an animal's life. Tracks and trails deserve to be preserved, both to increase your knowledge and as a record you can share with others. Preservation is commonly made in the form of written notes, casts, or photographs.

Perhaps the most important item in the naturalist's tool kit is the field notebook. Field notes can jog the memory and facilitate better retention of knowledge. The notes can be analyzed later and can be preserved as records of chance encounters. Writing good field notes is an art form and a science in itself. Field notes are a source of pride when shown to others and may gain recognition for recording rare and unusual events. And need I mention how quickly memories, especially for details, fade when not preserved?

While great and complex systems have been designed for complete and accurate records, there are really but three requirements for the tracker: ruler, paper, and pen. With these, every trail becomes a record for later analysis and sharing. I cannot emphasize enough the importance of enhancing your tracking experience by keeping notes to which you can later refer!

A simple 3-by-5-inch notebook and a 6-inch ruler are adequate to get started. Use a pencil or a pen that won't run if your notes get wet. To facilitate taking notes, A Naturalist's

World produces a waterproof notebook that contains information about footprint groups, gaits, and how to track; data sheets for recording information; and English and metric rulers imprinted on the back cover. See the Introduction for contact information for A Naturalist's World.

Tracks may also be preserved by photographing and making casts. Good photographs can be made by any modern camera that can take a good close-up. When taking pictures, try to fill the viewfinder with the footprint. Get as close as possible. Always include a ruler or some other object in the photo to provide a sense of scale. Avoid using hats, gloves, hands, or objects without a straight edge; round edges do not lend themselves to making accurate measurements from a photo. To avoid distortion, take the photograph from directly above the track, shooting straight down. Also, step back and take photographs of the trail to show the footprints that were photographed close-up. Fast films (ASA of 200 or higher) are generally best, because tracks are often found in dark places, especially ground surfaces.

Plaster casts are the old standby for preserving tracks. I suggest a casting kit that includes a 1-gallon (4-liter) plastic jar with a screw lid for carrying dry plaster, a narrow spatula, a plastic mixing cup such as those sold for medium-sized drinks, paper for wrapping and transporting the finished cast, and a plastic sack for cleanup. A bottle of water may be needed if water is not available on site. Two pounds of plaster will make at least four coyote-sized track casts.

Purchase plaster from a lumberyard or hardware store, as prices will be more reasonable than at a drugstore or hobby shop. Almost any plaster will work, including plaster of paris, hydrocal, ultracal, or hydrostone. Avoid getting plaster for wallboard or patching compound, however. These plasters are formulated to be slightly flexible on walls and do not get hard enough for casts.

Two factors are critical to preventing casts from breaking: thickness and density. In the field, thickness is assured by building a wall around the track to contain the plaster. Natural objects such as twigs, stones, and dirt may be used to make a retaining wall 0.25–0.5 in (0.6–1.3 cm) above the track. Alternatively, walls in the form of plastic strips cut from milk cartons or other plastic containers may be brought to the field. Proper density is assured by mixing two parts of plaster to one part of water by volume (read instructions on plaster container) to create a mixture similar in consistency to thick pancake batter or a milkshake.

Place your spatula close to the track and pour onto the spatula to break the fall of the plaster into the footprint. Working quickly, so the plaster does not set and become too thick, gently pour the plaster first into the fine detailed areas of the footprint and then the rest of the print. Finally, pour the plaster to an appropriate depth (inside the retaining wall) to keep the cast from breaking. Vibrating the spatula up and down across the top of the plaster will cause it to settle evenly and create a smooth back for the cast.

Allow the plaster to dry for 30 minutes, or as long as is recommended on the plaster package. Gently pick the plaster up by digging your fingers under opposite sides of the cast, and turn the cast over onto one hand. Now wash off the dirt by rubbing the cast with your fingertips under the flowing water of a stream or a hose. Do not wash the cast in a sink as it may clog the drain. Let the cast continue to cure for several days in a warm, dry environment. If you need to transport it, wrap the cast in paper. Never wrap it in plastic as trapped moisture may cause it to crumble.

While special techniques are needed for dust and snow, this procedure will allow casting in many situations. Remember, carry a plastic garbage bag and *always* clean up your mess. No sign of your plaster should remain to reduce the experience of others who happen by later.

Scats and bird pellets

Scats and bird pellets (also called cough pellets or castings) are often helpful for identifying an animal or completing the story written in the trail. Scats and pellets help identify not only what the animal was eating, but who the animal was. However, it should be noted that scats and pellets won't help you identify an animal with as much certainty as tracks will. Many animals make similar scats and pellets that are difficult to tell apart.

The scats of many carnivores are very similar, especially when the diet is mostly meat. Size alone does not provide a definitive answer because of the wide range of diameters produced within a species and even by a single member of a species. For example, fox produce scats ranging in size from 0.3–0.8 in (0.8–2 cm), coyotes produce scats from 0.5–1.3 in (1.3–3.3 cm), and wolves produce scats from 0.5–1.5 in (1.3–3.8 cm), and we all know how our own scat varies in size and shape. When judging size, consider both the total quantity of scat and the size of individual pieces. Moist food produces slimmer scats, while fibrous diets produce wider scats.

Given these cautions, scat shapes can be used to identify general groups of animals (see page xii). Spherical shapes flattened top to bottom are deposited by members of the rabbit order. Elongate spheres are deposited by rodents and shrews, and at larger sizes by deer and their relatives. Long, thick cords are deposited by dogs, bears, and raccoons. Dog scats typically have tapered ends, while those from bears and raccoons are blunt. Cats also produce thick cords with blunt ends, but they tend to be constricted or even broken into short segments. Cords that loop back on themselves are produced by members of the weasel family. Birds, in general, produce long, thin cords or shapeless, semiliquid excretions. Reptiles and amphibians may produce small elongate spheres or long, thin cords. White, nitrogenous urine deposits, found only on the scats of birds, reptiles, and amphibians, separate them from mammal scats.

Scats may be confused with cough pellets. Many bird groups, including owls, raptors, crows, ravens, jays, magpies, gulls, herons, storks, flycatchers, and kingfishers, produce cough pellets in addition to scats. Birds pass digestive juices through what they have eaten to remove the nutrients. Hair, bones, beaks, claws, and other non-digestible parts accumulate in the gizzard (anterior portion of stomach), are compressed, and are coughed up as pellets. Food remnants in the pellet are easy to identify and tell much about the bird's feeding habits and even the habitats it frequents.

cough pellet

Pellets are grayish in color and are spherical or long and tapered at both ends. When fresh, they are covered by mucus and appear dark black. Pellets are found mainly at roosting sites and nests, and occasionally at feeding areas. They are deposited singly, but many may accumulate beneath a tree where a bird is roosting, nesting, or perching. Nitrogenous scat deposits on the ground or twigs may help verify an object as a pellet.

The diameter of the throat determines the maximum diameter of the pellet. In general, large birds produce larger pellets. Shape and diameter allow one to distinguish to some degree between species.

Birds generally produce two pellets per day and regurgitate just before taking flight. The time of day when feeding occurred may affect the sample of food items. For example, owls tend to feed on mammals that come out only at night, while hawks feed on animals that are out during the daylight hours.

Shapes of scats

Spheres

Rabbits and their relatives

rabbit

Spheres, elongate

Rodents, shrews, armadillo, deer, and their relatives

 woodrat

shrew

elk

Cords, long and thick

Coyotes, bears, raccoons, and their relatives

coyote

bear

raccoon

Cords, thick and often constricted

Mountain lions and their relatives

mountain lion

Cords, often folded

Weasels and their relatives

mink

Cords, long and thin, often with nitrogenous deposits

Birds and reptiles

Canada goose

lizard

Anatomy and footprint nomenclature

The feet of mammals, birds, reptiles, and amphibians are anatomically complex, and that complexity shows in their footprints. Knowing something of the anatomy of their feet will aid in footprint identification and interpreting trails.

The toes of all animals are numbered from the inside of the foot out (the inside of the foot being the side closest to the animal). Therefore, in humans and other mammals, the thumb or big toe (if present) is number 1 and the little finger or little toe is number 5. In birds, toe 1 (if present) points backward.

Over evolutionary time, toes of animals have become reduced in size or have disappeared altogether. In cats and dogs, toe 1 is absent or reduced to a small toe called a *dewclaw*. In deer, elk, sheep, and similar mammals, toe 1 is absent and toes 2 and 5 are reduced and form dewclaws. Toes 3 and 4, the *clouts*, form the cloven *hoof*. In pronghorn antelope, toes 1, 2, and 5 are absent. In birds, toe 5 is absent and toe 1 is often reduced, and occasionally is absent. In the amphibians covered here, toe 1 has been lost from the front foot.

Track measurements

To more accurately determine the animal's foot size from its tracks, mountain lion researchers Fjelline and Mansfield (1989) developed the "minimum outline" method of measuring tracks.

Place your hand on a hard surface, a table for instance. Note the contact area of your hand with that surface. If your hand went no deeper into that surface, your handprint would have only one size—the *minimum outline*. If your hand were to sink deeper into the surface—as it would if the surface were, say, mud—it would create a series of variable outlines, each larger than the one before, as the mud flowed around the curved surface of your hand. All footprints have a minimum outline, but only prints that sink into a surface have variable outlines.

Note that while the variable outline of a footprint may only be several millimeters wider than the minimum outline, those few millimeters have a large visual effect. The human eye sees area, and area increases with the square of a linear measurement. In short, a few millimeters of width adds a lot of area to a footprint.

The minimum outline size does not change for different surfaces, and therefore provides a standard for comparison between surfaces. And though one animal may leave many sizes of footprints depending on surface, slope, and speed, there is only one minimum outline for every footprint an animal might leave. The minimum outline measurement is the only constant and consistent size in tracking.

To measure the minimum outline, study the bottom of a print. The *break point* where the rounded pad turns upward is the edge of the minimum outline. Use this edge to measure tracks.

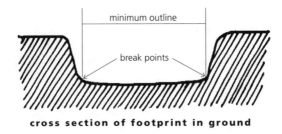

cross section of footprint in ground

Assigning the break point is a subjective judgment and no two people will always mark it at exactly the same point. However, testing has shown that an individual tracker using the minimum outline method can reduce personal variation in measurement and that groups of trackers using this method will also become more consistent in their measurement of tracks. Quality measurements are the tracker's goal, and using minimum outline methods greatly reduces over-exaggeration and variance in measurement.

All measurements in this guide are minimum outline measurements.

The measurements in *Scats and Tracks of the Desert Southwest* are mostly averages gathered from years of tracking. Averages include only animals judged to be adult. However, it is important to remember the great size variation among animals. Every animal was small once in its life, and some never get big. Males are often substantially larger than females. Regional variations in mammal sizes also occur. For example, coyotes are smaller in the southwestern United States and larger in the northeastern part of the country. Their tracks vary accordingly. Therefore, a track in the field may be considerably larger or smaller than the measurements provided. Use track measurements only as a rough guideline, not as an absolute rule.

Gaits and trails

Coordinated muscle movements result in the various gaits used by animals. In the simplest form, when moving on two legs (bipedal movement) an organism can *walk, run,* and *hop.* When moving on four legs (quadrupedal movement) an organism can *walk, trot, lope, gallop, bound,* and *pronk* (also called *stot*). Though other gaits exist, we will confine our discussion to these basics. Each gait leaves a characteristic pattern that may be modified by changes in speed and body angle. The combination of footprints is called the *trail.* The bipedal walk and run and the quadrupedal walk and trot result in gaits that are *symmetrical.* The right side of the trail is a mirror image of the left side. The trail patterns for these gaits are the same, alternating right-left pattern, and they differ only by the stride being longer in the run and trot than it is in the walk. In the run and trot, the straddle, the distance from the right edge of the rightmost pad (see page xix) to the left edge of the leftmost pad, also tends to be narrower than it is in the walk.

Quadrupedal movement also results in gaits that are *asymmetrical* (the right half of the trail is *not* always a mirror image of the left), including lope, gallop, bound, hop, and pronk. These gaits produce patterns that include all four footprints (two fronts, two hinds, two rights, and two lefts) in a group separated from the next group by a space where no footprints appear.

walk   **trot**

In *gallops*, the feet, front and rear, that move first (or *lead*) will determine whether the gallop will form a Z-shaped or C-shaped pattern. When the front and hind feet on the same side lead, the pattern takes on a Z shape. A right front lead with a left hind lead or vice versa results in a C-shaped pattern. Thus, there are four possible gallop patterns.

C-shaped gallop   **Z-shaped gallop**

Bounds (also known as hops and jumps) are characterized by the synchronization of the hind feet; both strike the ground at the same time, side by side. The front feet strike the ground at a different time than the hind feet. In a full bound, the front feet are synchronized and strike the ground side by

full bound   **half bound**

side at the same time. In a half bound, only the hind feet are synchronized and the front feet hit the ground staggered. Animals that mostly use full bounds, also called hops, live in trees (tree squirrels and songbirds), whereas those that mostly use half bounds live on the ground (ground squirrels and rabbits).

In a *pronk* (also called a *stot*), all four feet strike the ground at the same time, with the front feet side by side and forward of the hind feet, which are also side by side. This gait is often used by deer to gain height and increase time in the air to look around.

To increase peripheral vision, non-primate mammals have eyes placed toward the side of their heads, not flat on their face like humans. By turning sideways, a prey species can see what is pursuing it and where it needs to go to escape. The predator, by turning sideways, can see what it is chasing and where the rest of the predator pack is.

slow side trot

side gallop

Consequently, quadrupedal mammals have evolved to use all gaits while their body is turned to the side. These *side gaits* result when the animal's heavy head deviates from the line of travel and the body turns sideways. First, the front feet respond by moving toward the side of the trail where the head is. Then, as the head turns more, the hind feet move to the side away from the head. The greater the head movement, the greater the angle of the side gait. Common examples are the side trot and side gallop often used by canids. These are often called a dog trot or dog gallop.

An animal's size is also reflected in its gait patterns. When a mammal is walking with its normal gait, for example, the stride is 1.1 to 1.25 times larger than the distance from the hip to the shoulder joint. Using this crude relationship, body size can be judged from a walking stride. A 22-in stride indicates a hip-to-shoulder length of 20 in. Add to the hip-to-shoulder distance an estimate for the head length beyond the shoulder joint and an estimate of the rump length beyond the hip joint to get a total estimate of animal body length.

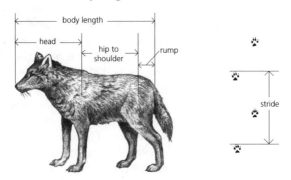

estimating mammal length from stride

Speed also modifies gait patterns in trails. There are three rules governing how pattern changes as speed changes:

1. As speed increases, the hind foot lands farther forward than the front footprint on the same side. Conversely, as speed decreases, the hind foot lands farther back in relation to the front footprint.

2. As speed increases, stride increases.

3. As speed increases, straddle usually decreases.

Speed changes are easily observed in quadrupedal walk and trot trail patterns. As speed increases, the hind footprint registers in front of the front print. This faster version of a walk is called an amble. The faster version of a trot doesn't have a name. When the animal slows to the point that the hind feet are registering behind the front prints, the animal may be stalking something. Trots are

**walk
(slower)**

**amble
(faster)**

front track large, hind small

| 1 x 2 x 1 lope | 2 x 2 lope | 3 x 3 lope |

separated from walks by having a stride two or more times greater than the estimated hip-to-shoulder distance of an animal.

A slow version of the gallop is also recognizable. When a gallop slows to the point that one or more hind feet register behind the leading edge of the frontmost footprint in a group pattern, the gait is called a *lope*. The gait is still a gallop, it's just a slow gallop.

Trail measurements

The terms *stride, group, intergroup,* and *straddle* describe the size of an animal trail. The *stride* is measured from the point where a foot touches the ground surface to where the same point of the same foot next touches the surface, and consists of one group and one intergroup measurement. The *group* consists of all four footprints (two fronts, two hinds, two lefts, two rights), while the *intergroup* is the distance between groups. Gait patterns take their name from the configuration of the group. The stride provides an indication of size in a walking animal and an indication of relative speed for other gaits (see pages xvii and xviii).

The *straddle* indicates the width of the trail and is measured from the outside rightmost pad of the outside right footprint of a group to the outside leftmost pad footprint of the same group. The outside edges of the trail are used because the inside of footprints overlap for many carnivore species.

Stride, group, and intergroup are all measured parallel to the trail, while the straddle is measured at right angles to the trail. Select a straight section of trail on level ground to measure. The slightest curve in the trail will distort the straddle measurement.

Glossary of terms

amble: a fast walk in which the hind footprint registers anterior to the front footprint. See illustration on page xviii.

asymmetrical: not symmetrical, that is, one side is not a mirror image of the opposite side.

bound: a *gait* in which both hind feet strike the ground at the same time, side by side. If the front feet also land side by side, the motion is said to be a *full bound*. A *half bound* occurs when one front foot strikes the ground in front of the other. See illustration on page xvi.

clout: term used to refer to toe 3 or toe 4 of the hoof. See illustration on page xxiv.

convergent toes: Toes 2 and 4 of ducks, geese, and swans, which bend toward the *foot axis,* especially at the tips. Compare to *divergent toes.*

cord: See *scat shape.*

cough pellet: remnants of bones and hair coughed up by many bird species after feeding on prey.

dewclaw: toe that over evolutionary time has become reduced in size and raised on the leg, away from the other toes. For example, toe 1 in dogs and toes 2 and 5 in deer.

diagnostic: providing certain identification of an animal or its sign.

digitigrade: walking on the tips of the toes. Dogs and cats, for example, are digitigrade. Tracks left by digitigrades rarely show a *sole.* Compare *plantigrade.*

digit: one of the toes of an animal.

digital pad: See *pad.*

distal webbing: See *webbing.*

divergent toes: Toes that are straight or turn out from the *foot axis* at the tips, specifically toes 2 and 4 of sea gulls. Compare to *convergent toes.*

foot axis: imaginary line down the center of the foot. It runs between toes 3 and 4 in deer and their relatives, and down toe 3 of other mammals. In birds, the foot axis also runs down toe 3.

fringe: webbing attached to a single toe. May have a smooth edge, known as a *simple fringe* or *simple lobe,* or it may be wavy, in which case it is said to have *indented lobes.*

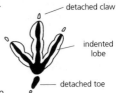

detached claw

indented lobe

detached toe

full bound: See *bound.*

gait: term for the type(s) of movement an animal uses when moving. Examples of gaits include *walk, amble, trot, bound,* and *gallop.* Gaits are defined by the mechanics of body movement, not by speed.

gallop: a *gait* in which hind feet move around the front feet and (usually) strike the ground in front of the front feet. Galloping forms distinct *group* patterns (two fronts, two hinds, two lefts, two rights) separated by an intergroup distance from the next set of four feet. Gallops fall into two basic patterns: Z-shaped and C-shaped.

group: a subunit of a *stride* including four footprints (two fronts and two hinds, and two lefts and two rights). The measure of the group plus the intergroup equals the measure of the stride.

half bound: See *bound.*

heel: portion of foot or track to the rear of digital and interdigital *pads.* In mammals, may be covered with hair, naked (without hair), or have one or more proximal pads. In reptiles and amphibians, may be textured with *tubercles.*

hop: synonymous with *bound,* often used in reference to *gaits* of rodents and rabbits.

indented lobe: See *fringe.*

interdigital pad: See *pad.*

length: of a *track,* the distance from front of toe *pads* to back of the interdigital pads, measured parallel to the *foot axis.* In mammal tracks, does not include claws. In bird tracks, does not include toe 1, but includes claws if they are attached and indistinguishable from toe pad.

line of travel: imaginary line on the ground over which the center of gravity of an animal passes.

lobe: See *fringe.*

lope: a slow *gallop,* in which at least one hind foot registers behind a front foot in a group of four footprints. See illustration on page xix.

mesial webbing: See *webbing.*

minimum outline: See pages xiii–xiv for extended discussion.

nipple-dimple: See *scat shape.*

outer toe angle: in birds, the angle between toes 2 and 4. In perching birds less than 90° and in shorebirds greater than 120°.

oval: See *scat shape.*

pad: hard, callus-like structure on the sole of an animal's foot. Each toe may have a digital pad. One or more interdigital pads are located directly to the rear of the toes, and one or more proximal pads may be located directly to the rear of the interdigital pads. In deer and their relatives, there is a single pad separated from the *wall* by the 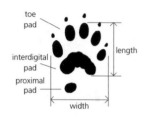 subunguinis. In birds, a metatarsal pad may occur directly under the leg bone.

plantigrade: walking on the soles of the foot. Raccoons, bears, and humans, for example, are plantigrade. The *sole* of the foot usually shows in the footprint. Compare *digitigrade.*

pronk: a *gait* in which all four feet strike the ground simultaneously and directly below the body. The *group* pattern shows two front footprints ahead of the two hind prints. Also called a *stot.* See illustration on page xvii.

proximal pad: See *pad.*

proximal webbing: See *webbing.*

rotatory gallop: a type of *gallop* which tends to form a C-shaped *group* pattern. See illustration on page xvi.

run: a *gait* used when moving only on two legs. It differs from a *walk* in having a longer *stride.*

scat shape: *Cords* are long pieces of scat, typically four to ten times longer than the width. Ends may be blunt or tapered. *Ovals* are pieces of scat typically two to four times longer than wide and tapered at both ends. A *"nipple-dimple"*–shaped scat pellet has a point at one end and a depression at the other. See chart on page xii.

simple fringe, simple lobe: See *fringe.*

sole: bottom of an animal's foot. It may be covered with hair or naked, and may have one or more *pads* on it.

stot: See *pronk.*

straddle: the distance from the right edge of the rightmost *pad* to the leftmost edge of the leftmost pad in a *trail.* Measured at right angles to the *line of travel.*

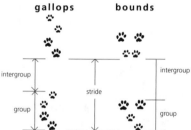

stride: The distance from the point where a foot touches the ground to the point where the same same foot touches the ground again. Measured parallel to the *line of travel.* One stride is equal to a *group* plus an intergroup measurement.

subunguinis: the soft material under the nails of humans. In deer and their relatives, refers specifically to the soft material between the *pad* and *wall.*

symmetrical: having two sides, one the mirror image of the other side.

toe pad: See *pad.*

track: refers to an individual footprint. Some measurable characteristics include *length* and *width.*

track pattern: the gross visual image of the pattern of footprints on the ground. A repeating pattern of two prints separated from the next two is called "two-by" and written 2 x 2. Prints may also show patterns of 3 x 3, 4 x 4, and 1 x 2 x 1. These patterns are made during a *gallop* or a *bound.* A few of these patterns are illustrated on page xix.

trail: a series of footprints and associated sign that marks the passage of an animal. Some measurable characteristics include *stride* and *straddle*.

transverse gallop: a type of *gallop* which tends to form a Z-shaped *group* pattern. See illustration on page xvi.

trot: a *gait* in which evenly spaced footprints alternate on right and left sides of the *line of travel*. Hind footprint registers on top of front. As speed increases, hind moves forward of front. Same patterns as a *walk*, but longer *stride*. May be done with body turned to side. See illustration on page xvii.

tubercle: rough pinhead-sized protuberance on the *sole* of the foot of a reptile or amphibian.

fast
trot

unguinis: hard material forming nails in humans, hoof walls in deer and their relatives, and claws in other mammals. Composed of hair pasted together by body glues.

walk: a *gait* where evenly spaced footprints alternate on right and left sides of the *line of travel*. Hind footprint registers on top of front. As speed increases, hind moves forward of front. See illustrations on pages xvi and xviii.

wall: hard material around the edge of each clout of a hoof. Technically the *unguinis,* which also forms human nails and animal claws.

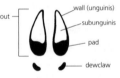

webbing: thin membrane stretched between toes of animals. The webbing may be near the tips of the toes *(distal)*, about midway to the toe tips *(mesial)*, or attached at the base *(proximal)*. A membrane attached to only one toe is called a *fringe*.

width: of a *track,* the greatest distance from the right side of the *pads* of a foot to the left side, whether the greatest distance is across the toes or palm pads. Measured perpendicular to the *foot axis*. In bird tracks, includes claws if they are attached and indistinguishable from toe pad.

How to use *Scats and Tracks*

Scats and Tracks of the Desert Southwest is designed for easy use in the field. The gray bars found on the edges of the pages of the track accounts will help you measure scat diameter and footprint size; each of these bars is keyed to the average size of the sign in question. A ruler is provided on the back cover. Below, we provide the background knowledge that every tracker should be familiar with before going to the field or using this book. Please take some time to study this material.

Illustrations

Illustrator Todd Telander applied his great ability to my collection of plaster casts, photographs, and slides, "drawing" on my experience to produce the most up-to-date and accurate illustrations possible. These drawings—made from the best specimens in a collection of thousands—represent the culmination of decades of tracking experience and are far more accurate than the tracker usually finds in tracking books. The tracks you find on the ground may not have as much detail or be as clear, but it is better to have an excellent drawing to compare to an imperfect track than to have to compare a track to a drawing lacking critical details.

How to use the track accounts

The track accounts in this guide have been grouped by similar footprint characteristics. Each track account represents a single species or a group of species with similar track characteristics. Each account is presented across a two-page spread, and is conveniently divided into sections as discussed below.

A brief listing of visual characteristics used to identify an animal begins each track account, appearing beneath the common and scientific names of the species. These descriptions are general, and great variability of pattern can exist among animals in the field. We recommend consulting appropriate field identification guides.

Track: A concise description of key points of footprints, to be used for identification. The accompanying track illustrations are not at actual size, but, unless otherwise noted, actual (average) length of the footprint is shown as a bar on the right side of the right-hand page. Average width is shown as a bar on the bottom of the right-hand page. In the field, place the appropriate measurement bar next to the track to compare size. To take a numerical measurement, use the ruler printed on the back cover of the book.

The tracks illustrated are all from right feet, except in the entries for birds, where both feet are pictured. Numerical measurements are given in the form *length* x *width*. Note that measurements of mammal tracks do not include claws, that measurements of bird tracks include claws but do not include toe 1, and that measurements generally do not include parts of the foot which often do not register in a given species's track (e.g., heels in the hind feet of some rodent species).

Trail: The average size of the stride of the most commonly used gait or gaits is given. Other common or characteristic gaits, if any, are discussed. See *track pattern* in the Glossary of Terms on page xxiii. For more information on gaits in tracking, see my *Field Guide to Mammal Tracking in North America*. Gaits are displayed up the right side of the right-hand page. If the common gait is a walk or trot, however, it may not be illustrated, since all walking and trotting patterns consist of right-left alternating patterns.

Scat: A description of scat supplements the drawing. Average scat width is shown as a bar up the side of the left-hand page. In the field, place the appropriate measurement bar next to the scat to compare sizes. To take a numerical measurement, use the ruler printed on the back cover of the book. Numerical measurements of scat are given under the illustrations in the form *length* x *width*. In cases of small scat, only width is given; thus, a single measurement always indicates diameter.

Habitat: To aid in locating and differentiating tracks, the animal's habitat preferences are listed. Some animals with large ranges, such as the beaver, are only found in specific habitats.

Similar species: Clues are provided to help differentiate an animal's tracks from similar tracks of other species. With these clues, identification should be possible.

Other sign: Other sign of animals, besides tracks and scat, are listed or illustrated to help with identification, and simply to provide more information on animal lives.

In addition, a distribution map is provided with each account. This gives a generalized picture of where in the Southwest region an animal may be found. Animals that require specific habitats will of course not be evenly distributed through the shown range.

To make the best use of this guide, carry it with you into the field. When you come across an unfamiliar track or trail, open the book to the appropriate track account and place the page alongside the track for immediate on-site comparison.

Visual key to tracks

This simple key includes birds, reptiles, amphibians, and mammals. It is arranged by the number of toes that show in a good footprint, ranging from two toes to five toes. Those animals that show four toes in the front print and five toes in the hind are listed between four- and five-toed animals.

Snakes (pp. 8–9)

Series of side-to-side trail undulations.

Deer and Relatives (pp. 130–141)

Two toes form hard, cloven hoof. Dewclaws may show in deep print.

Birds with Webbed Feet (pp. 18–33)

Three toes facing forward, often a fourth toe facing backward. Claws may be detached from toes. Webbing between two or more toes.

Birds without Webbed Feet (pp. 34–53)

Three toes facing forward, often a fourth toe facing backward. Claws may be detached from toes.

Wolves, Dogs, and Relatives (pp. 60–67)

Four toes in front and hind prints. Claws usually present and detached. Single anterior lobe on interdigital pad.

Cougars, Cats, and Relatives (pp. 68–77)

Four toes in front and hind prints. Claws usually absent. Double anterior lobe on interdigital pad.

Rabbits and Relatives (pp. 94–97)

Four toes in front and hind footprint. An exceptionally clear print may show a fifth inner toe in the front footprint. Pads lacking, bottom of foot covered with hair. Long hopping heel in hind print.

Rodents (pp. 98–129)

Most have four toes in front prints and five in hind. Beaver has five toes in front print. Front toes show a 1-2-1 grouping, hind show a 1-3-1 grouping. Long hopping heel in hind print.

Armadillo (pp. 58–59)

Four toes in front print and five in hind. Often only the prominent inner toes, 2 on front, 3 on rear, register.

Salamanders (pp. 2–3)

Four toes in front print, five toes in hind. Trail wide, often with a tail drag.

Frogs (pp. 4–5)

Four toes in front print, five toes in hind. Long, slender toes. Front print faces center of trail. Distal webbing in hind print.

Toads (pp. 6–7)

Four toes in front print, five toes in hind. Front print faces center of trail. Mesial webbing in hind print. Tubercles may show on front and hind prints.

American Alligator (pp. 16–17)

Five toes on front foot. Inside and outside toes are opposite and form a straight line. Four toes on hind foot with a well-developed heel. Claws detached.

Snapping Turtle (pp. 14–15)

Five toes show in front and hind tracks. Front prints toe-in and hind prints may toe-out. Feet are relatively broad. Claws robust and often visible. Sometimes the claws are the only visible signs on hard ground.

Lizards (pp. 10–13)

Five toes in front and hind prints. Toes long and slender. Claws may be detached. Tail drag often present in trail.

Opossum   (pp. 54–55)

Five toes. Distinct hind print with an opposable (like human thumb) inside toe protruding sideways from other toes. Outside toe is slightly separated from middle three toes.

Shrew (pp. 56–57)

Five slender toes present on front and hind feet. In clear prints, four interdigital and two proximal pads may be seen.

Raccoons and Relatives (pp. 80–85)

Five toes in front and hind prints. Toes often round or bulbous at ends. May have long, slender toes.

Weasels and Relatives   (pp. 86–93)

Five toes in front and hind prints, though the little toe (on inside of foot) may not show. Toes in a 1-3-1 grouping. Interdigital pad is chevron-shaped. Plantigrade hind foot.

Black Bear (pp. 78–79)

Five toes in front and hind prints, though the little toe (on inside of foot) may not show. Toes evenly spaced. Plantigrade hind foot.

Scats
and
Tracks
of the

Desert Southwest

Tiger Salamander

Ambystoma tigrinum

Hot dog–sized
salamander, up
to 9 in (23 cm)
long. Moist,
smooth skin.
Body brown to
black to dark green,
with yellow spots or streaks. Tubercles on underside of
foot. The only salamander of the high mountains.

Track: Four toes on front foot (often only three show), and five
toes on hind foot. The outline of the
foot may not show, just toe prints.
Even in a clear print, tubercles rarely
show.

Trail: Walking stride is about 3 in
(7.5 cm). Trail has a wide straddle
relative to stride, and may show oscillating belly and tail drag marks.

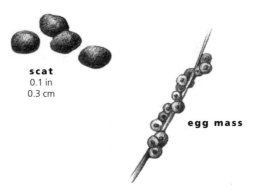

scat
0.1 in
0.3 cm

egg mass

SCAT WIDTH

Scat: Soft, pea-sized black masses with some hint of oval shape.

Habitat: Quiet waters around lakes, ponds, and streams in grassland meadow areas and forests. Found to 9,200 ft (2,760 m).

Similar species: Differs from lizards by wider, oscillating tail drag and by having only four toes on front foot.

Other sign: Eggs in egg masses are attached individually to underwater plant stems.

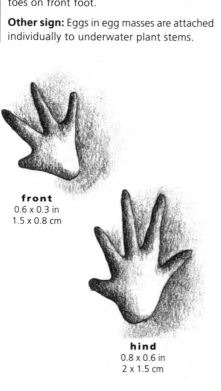

front
0.6 x 0.3 in
1.5 x 0.8 cm

hind
0.8 x 0.6 in
2 x 1.5 cm

amble

FRONT TRACK LENGTH

FRONT TRACK WIDTH

Chorus Frog
Pseudacris triseriata

Silver dollar–sized frog less than 1.5 in (3.8 cm). Color variable from brown to green body with three dark stripes on back. Dark stripe through eye to rump. Middle stripe may fork into two stripes near rump. The two subspecies found in this range, *P. t. triseriata* Western Chorus Frog and *P. t. maculata* Boreal Chorus Frog, vary in color patterns.

Track: Four toes on front foot and five on hind. Front feet face in. Four hind toes face in, with one facing out. Proximal webbing on hind feet extending at most one-quarter of way out to toe tips.

Trail: Hopping stride about 10 in (25 cm). Frogs may easily hop 3 ft (1 m) when in a hurry.

scat
0.4 x 1.25 in
1 x 3.3 cm

egg mass and tadpole

Scat: Black, firm cord with slightly tapering ends.

Habitat: Shallow water with emergent vegetation including pond and lake shores, marshes and beaver ponds.

Similar species: Lack the palm tubercles of the front feet of toad. Less webbing between toes. Hop more and longer distances. Smaller than southern leopard frog *Rana sphenocephala*.

Other sign: Inconspicuous egg masses consisting of a few eggs in a packet attached to vegetation below water line.

walk

front
0.4 x 0.4 in
1 x 1 cm

proximal web

hind
0.8 x 0.6 in
2 x 1.5 cm

hop

FRONT TRACK LENGTH

FRONT TRACK WIDTH

Woodhouse's Toad

Bufo woodhousei

Baseball-sized toad, up to 5 in (7.5 cm) long. Body is light brown to gray to green, with warty skin and dark spots. A white line runs down the back. Female larger than male.

Track: Four toes on front foot and five on hind. Front feet face in. Tubercles on heel of front foot. Four hind toes face in, while one faces out. Two tubercles may show on the heel of the hind foot and can be confused with toes. Webbing, found only on hind feet, extends at most halfway out to toe tips.

Trail: Walking stride is about 3 in (7.5 cm). Hopping stride generally less than 1 ft (0.3 m).

scat
1 x 0.3 in
2.5 x 0.8 cm

egg mass

toad imprint in mud

SCAT WIDTH

Scat: Dark brown to black. Long cord, up to five times longer than wide. Sometimes contains insect parts.

Habitat: Lakes, ponds, beaver ponds.

Similar species: Differs from frogs by presence of tubercles on front heels. Hind foot is narrower than frog. Walks and uses short hops more than the usually long-hopping frog.

Other sign: Long strings of egg masses on pond and lake bottoms and floating among vegetation.

walk

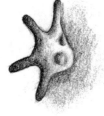

front
0.9 x 0.6 in
2.2 x 1.5 cm

mesial web

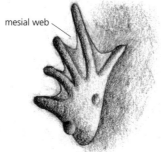

hind
1.1 x 0.9 in
2.8 x 2.2 cm

hop

FRONT TRACK LENGTH

FRONT TRACK WIDTH

Snakes
various species

Prairie rattlesnake
Crotalus viridis

A variety of
snakes, from
garter snakes
(*Thamnophis* **spp.**)
to rubber boas *(Charina bottae)* to bullsnakes
(Pituophis catenifer) to prairie rattlesnakes *(Crotalus viridis)*.

Track: No footprint to describe.

Trail: Varies from 1–4 in (2.5–10 cm)
wide. Characterized by side-to-side
undulations of the trail. The period,
the distance from one curve to the
next, varies by species, age, and
speed of the snake. Surface material is usually pushed up at the outside of each curve. Gait is either a
side-to-side undulation or sidewinding.

scat
4 x 0.4 in
10 x 1 cm

shed skin

Scat: Black or brown cord, with constrictions and undulations. White nitrogenous material often attached.

Habitat: Varies widely, from water's edge to rock outcrops to dry sand dunes.

Similar species: Resembles no other track.

Other sign: Shed skin.

**lateral
undulatory**

sidewinding

trail

Eastern Fence Lizard
Sceloporus undulatus

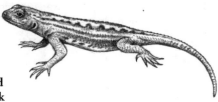

Roughly the size of a roll of Life Savers; body about 3 in (7.5 cm), with dry skin and ridged scales. Gray to dark brown above, with black crossbars or longitudinal stripes. Blue patches on side of throat. Considerable subspecies variation.

Track: Five relatively long, thin toes on front and hind feet. Hind heel is relatively long. Claws may show.

Trail: Trotting stride is about 3 in (7.5). Hind feet mostly register on top of front feet. Relatively wide straddle. Straight tail drag.

Scat: Brown cord, six to eight times longer than wide. White nitrogenous material usually found on one end.

scat
1.5 x 0.25 in
3.8 x 0.6 cm

Habitat: Wide variety of habitats including forests, woodland, prairie, and rock outcrops. Shelters in bushes, trees, under rock, or in logs.

Similar species: Differs from salamanders by having five narrow toes on front feet and straight tail drag.

Other sign: Scuff marks in dust may indicate a dust bath.

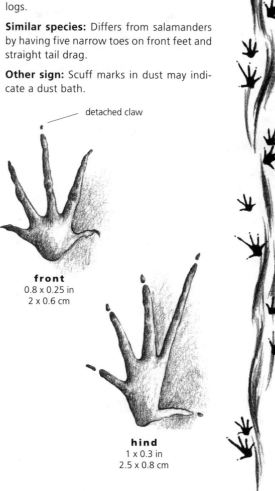

detached claw

front
0.8 x 0.25 in
2 x 0.6 cm

hind
1 x 0.3 in
2.5 x 0.8 cm

amble

FRONT TRACK LENGTH

FRONT TRACK WIDTH

Short-horned Lizard

Phrynosoma douglassi

Roughly the size of a calling card; body and tail less than 4 in (10 cm) long. Body relatively broad, with short horns projecting from back of head. A single row of fringe scales along edge of body. Body mottled gray to brown to tan, closely matching local terrain colors.

Track: Five relatively long, thin toes on front and hind feet. Hind heel is relatively long. Claws may show.

Trail: Trotting stride is 3 in (7.5 cm). Hind feet mostly register on top of front feet. Relatively wide straddle. Relatively straight tail drag and often a wider body drag.

Scat: Brown pellets three to six times longer than wide; may be tapered. White nitrogenous material may be found on one end.

scat
1.5 x 0.25 in
3.8 x 0.6 cm

SCAT WIDTH

Habitat: Determined by presence of fine, loose soil interspersed with firm, sandy or rocky terrain. Found in prairies and open woodlands, from plains high into mountains.

Similar species: Differs from salamanders by having five narrow toes on front feet and relatively straight tail drag.

Other sign: Scuff marks in loose sand where the lizard buries itself for camouflage.

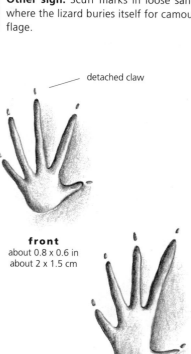

detached claw

front
about 0.8 x 0.6 in
about 2 x 1.5 cm

hind
about 1 x 0.6 in
about 2.5 x 1.5 cm

amble

FRONT TRACK LENGTH

FRONT TRACK WIDTH

Snapping Turtle

Chelydra serpentina

A large to very large turtle, weighing 8–12 lb (3.5–5.5 kg). The robust shell is lined by three toothed ridges. Large head with robust, hooked jaw. Tail longer than half the shell.

Track: Five toes show in front and hind tracks. Front prints toe-in and hind prints may toe-out. Feet are relatively broad. Claws robust and often visible. Sometimes the claws are the only visible signs on hard ground.

Trail: Walking stride ranges from 5–12 in (12.5–30 cm). Straddle is wide compared to stride. Tail drag often present.

scat
1.5 in
3.8 cm

Scat: Lacks well-defined shape. Color is algae green to dark black. Often soft.

Habitat: Always near water including swamps, marshes, lakes, streams, and rivers.

Similar species: Broad trail of five toed, clawed track with a tail drag separates the snapping turtle tracks and trail.

Other sign: I have not observed other sign.

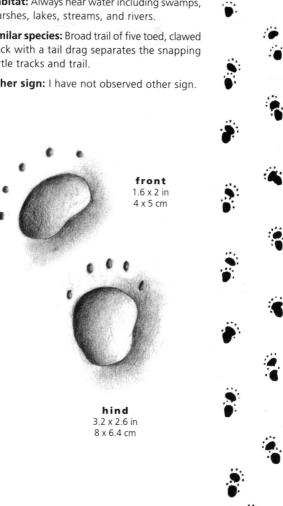

front
1.6 x 2 in
4 x 5 cm

hind
3.2 x 2.6 in
8 x 6.4 cm

walk

FRONT TRACK LENGTH

FRONT TRACK WIDTH

American Alligator

Alligator mississippiensis

**Adults range
in length
from 6–12 ft
(1.8–3.6 m).
Body color is black.
They have a rounded snout.**

Track: Five toes on front foot. Inside and outside toes are opposite and form a straight line. Four toes on hind foot with a well-developed heel. Claws detached. Skin tubercles may show in the bottom of the tracks. Tracks size varies considerably because alligators grow their whole life.

Trail: Walking stride is about 40 in (100 cm), but this varies with alligator size.

Scat: I have not observed their scat.

Habitat: Prefers river swamps, marshes, and bayous.

Similar species: No similar tracks for adults. Young might be confused with turtles, but have four toes on hind feet.

Other sign: Nest composed of vegetation and may be up to 7 ft (2.1 m) in diameter and 3 ft (90 cm) high.

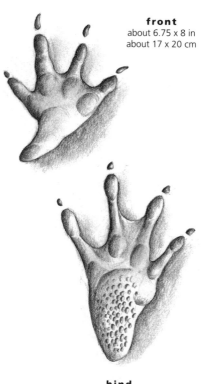

front
about 6.75 x 8 in
about 17 x 20 cm

hind
about 11 x 9 in
about 28 x 23 cm

walk

HALF FRONT TRACK LENGTH

HALF FRONT TRACK WIDTH

White Pelican
Pelecanus erythrorhynchos

Large aquatic bird, average length more than 60 in (150 cm), with a wingspan of more than 8 ft (2.4 m). White with black primary wing feathers. Large bill is yellow to orange.

Track: Four long, slender toes. Toe 1 offset to side of track. Feet *totipalmate,* with webbing between all four toes. Webbing distal and slightly convex between toes. Claws attached.

Trail: Walking stride averages 16 in (40 cm). Toes turn inward.

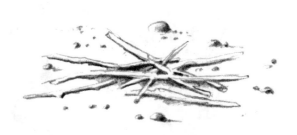

ground nest

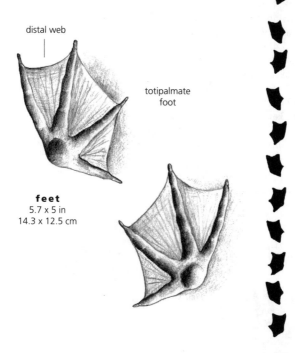

Scat: Shapeless, brownish white mass.

Habitat: Lakes, marshes, and bays. During summer, found in freshwater lakes; in winter, in salt water.

Similar species: Differs from all web-footed birds except cormorant by being totipalmate. Differs from cormorant by having attached claws.

Other sign: Nests on ground in large island colonies.

distal web

totipalmate
foot

feet
5.7 x 5 in
14.3 x 12.5 cm

walk

TRACK LENGTH

TRACK WIDTH

Great Blue Heron

Ardea herodias

Large wading bird, average length 45 in (113 cm). Gray-blue body, with white neck and yellow beak. Black crown extends on feathers off rear of head. Male and female similar in overall appearance.

Track: Four toes, toes 2–4 pointing forward. Small proximal web between toes 3 and 4. Footprint is asymmetrical, with toe 1 set to inside of foot axis (drawn through toe 3). Toe 1 is about 1.5 in (3.8 cm); toe 2 is longer than 1, though shorter than 3 and 4. On hard ground, metatarsal pad may not show and toes may appear unconnected.

Trail: Walking stride about 20 in (50 cm). Trail is fairly straight and feet point forward.

nest

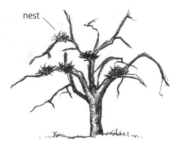

cough pellet   **rookery**

Scat: Semiliquid, predominantly white. Solid cords of scat vary from 2–3 in (5–7.5 cm) in length, and contain fish, frogs, salamanders, and even small rodents. Ground beneath nests becomes coated with droppings.

Habitat: Frequents backwater eddies along riverbanks and shallow edges of lakes.

Similar species: Differs from other shore-edge tracks by large size and asymmetrical placement of toes.

Other sign: Large colonies of nests high in trees. Undigested material may be coughed up as pellets.

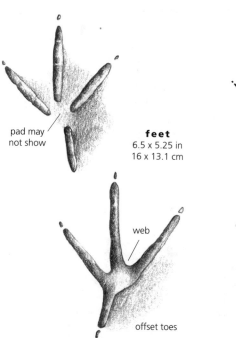

pad may not show

feet
6.5 x 5.25 in
16 x 13.1 cm

web

offset toes

walk

HALF TRACK LENGTH

HALF TRACK WIDTH

Sandhill Crane
Grus canadensis

**Large bird, average length
39 in (98 cm). Grayish, with
red crown on head, and
white cheeks and chin.
Appearance of males and
females similar.**

Track: Four toes, toes 2–4
showing. Outside toes op-
posed by nearly 180°. Toe 3
is longer than 2 and 4. Small
proximal web between toes 2
and 3 rarely shows. Claws usually
attached to toes, though claw of toe
1 rarely shows. Feet point forward.

Trail: Walking stride about 24 in
(60 cm). Often runs, extending its
stride. Tracks have a narrow straddle,
being nearly in line with one another.

Scat: Similar to, but smaller than,
Canada goose. Brown in color, with
some vegetation. Can contain bones
of small mammals, reptiles, and amphibians.

scat
2.5 x 0.3 in
6.3 x 0.8 cm

Habitat: Meadows, marshes, grasslands, and fields.

Similar species: Differs from ducks, geese, swans, and herons by having only small proximal web. Differs from large raptors by lacking toe 1.

Other sign: Listen for its rattling call, which suggests to some what dinosaurs may have sounded like.

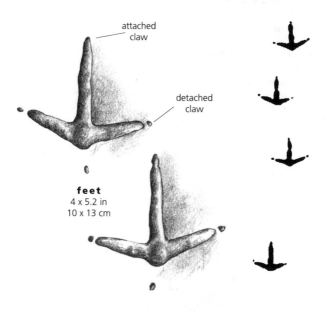

attached
claw

detached
claw

feet
4 x 5.2 in
10 x 13 cm

walk

Canada Goose
Branta canadensis

Medium-sized aquatic bird, average length 30 in (75 cm). Considerable size variation among subspecies. Black head and neck, with a white chin band. Back is olive brown. Male and female similarly colored.

Track: Four toes. Toes 2–4, which point forward, usually register. Toe 1 points rearward and only occasionally shows. Distal webbing between toes 2, 3, and 4. Toes 2 and 4 tend to converge slightly near tips. Claws are broad, blunt, and usually attached to toes. Feet turn in.

Trail: Walking stride is about 12 in (30 cm).

scat
3 x 0.4 in
7.5 x 1 cm

SCAT WIDTH

Scat: Cord, five to eight times longer than wide. Often greenish and coated with white nitrogenous deposits. As long as 3.5 in (8.8 cm).

Habitat: Ponds, lakes, marshes, streams, and rivers.

Similar species: Larger than most ducks and smaller than swans. Differs from pelican and cormorant by lacking webbing between toes 1 and 2. Size, convergent toes, and distal webbing differentiate them from gulls.

Other sign: Nests on ground, sometimes on cliff ledges, and in abandoned heron and raptor nests. Eggs larger than chicken eggs.

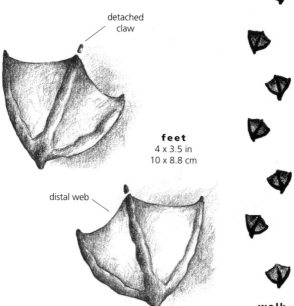

detached claw

feet
4 x 3.5 in
10 x 8.8 cm

distal web

walk

TRACK LENGTH

TRACK WIDTH

Ducks
various species

Aquatic birds with webbed feet, varying in size from the small bufflehead through mallards to pintails. Length ranges from 14–24 in (35–60 cm). Large variety in body patterns among species. Males generally more brightly colored than females.

Mallard
Anas platyrhynchos

Track: Four toes. Toes 2–4, which point forward, usually register. Toe 1 points rearward and may not show. Distal webbing between toes 2, 3, and 4. Webbing concave between toes. Toes 2 and 4 tend to converge near tips. Claws are broad, blunt, and attached to toes. Feet turned in.

Trail: Walking stride of a mallard *(Anas platyrhynchos)* is about 4 in (10 cm).

scat
2 x 0.25 in
5 x 0.8 cm

SCAT WIDTH

Scat: Pencil-sized cords, four to eight times longer than wide. Often greenish and coated with white nitrogen deposits.

Habitat: Ponds, lakes, marshes, streams, and rivers.

Similar species: Tracks smaller than geese and swan. Differ from pelicans and cormorants by lacking webbing between toes 1 and 2. Differ from gulls by having convergent toes.

Other sign: Nests may be on the ground, in tree cavities, or on floating mats. Eggs roughly the size of chicken eggs, though there may be great variation among species.

distal web

feet
2.2 x 2.4 in
5.5 x 6 cm

walk

TRACK LENGTH

TRACK WIDTH

Coot
Fulica americana

Medium-sized aquatic bird, average length 15 in (38 cm). Slate-black body, with white beak extending into small brown forehead shield.

Track: Four toes showing, toes 2–4 pointing forward. Toe 1 angles inward. Toes 2, 3, and 4 have fringe of webbing with indented lobes. Long, pointed claws, especially those on toe 1, may be separated from toes.

Trail: Walking stride 10 in (25 cm); tends to wander when walking. Foot axis parallel to line of travel.

Scat: White liquid.

Habitat: Freshwater lakes and ponds having shallow water where reeds and rushes grow.

Similar species: Differs from all other aquatic birds by the indented lobes on each toe.

Other sign: Floating nest built from cattails, sedges, and rushes, rising several inches above the water.

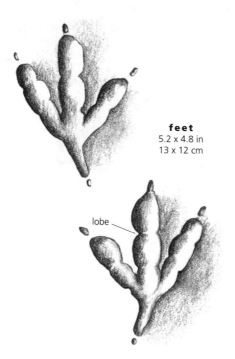

feet
5.2 x 4.8 in
13 x 12 cm

lobe

walk

TRACK LENGTH

HALF TRACK WIDTH

Shorebirds
various species

Many birds, such as sandpipers, killdeer, curlews, and snipes. Average length varies from 6–18 in (15–45 cm). All have similar footprints and differentiation is difficult.

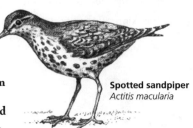

Spotted sandpiper
Actitis macularia

Track: Four narrow toes, although toe 1 may not show. Toes 2–4 face forward and are nearly symmetrical around toe 3. Outer toe angle often greater than 120°. Small, proximal webbing between toes 2, 3, and 4 may be visible, though curlews and sandpipers have proximal webbing only between toes 3 and 4.

Trail: Shorebirds are constantly running along the water's edge. Stride varies from 4–20 in (10–50 cm).

beach with beak holes

Scat: Small and semiliquid. Browns, green and white mixed.

Habitat: Water's edge at lakes, rivers, streams, wastewater treatment plants.

Similar species: Differ from song- or perching birds by the weak showing of toe 1, which in perching birds is strong and used to grasp branches. Outer toe angle of songbirds is less than 90°. Shorebirds walk, but most songbirds hop.

Other sign: Myriad roundish holes where beak pushed into the sand in pursuit of insects.

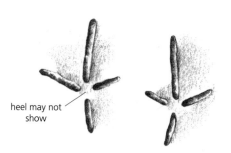

heel may not show

feet
1.25 x 1 in
3.1 x 2.5 cm

walk

Herring gull
Larus argentatus

**Large gull, average
length 25 in (63 cm).
Pale gray back, white
head. Tips of primary
feathers black. Yellow
bill with red spot;
pink legs.**

Track: Four toes. Toes 2–4 (forward-
pointing) show. Toe 1 may register only
slightly or not show at all. Webbing
relatively straight between toes. Toes
2 and 3 tend to diverge, especially at
the tips.

Trail: Walking stride is about 13 in
(33 cm). Feet turn slightly inward.

Scat: Semiliquid. Primarily white, with
indistinguishable contents.

cough pellet

Habitat: Along coast and on inland lakes and rivers. Nests in colonies on ground or cliffs, usually on islands. Nest is made of grass or seaweed. A scavenger, the herring gull is also found at dumps.

Similar species: Differs from ducks, swans, and geese by having divergent toes. Smaller than swans and geese. Differs from coot by having webbing between toes.

Other sign: Cough pellets containing bones, fish scales, urchin parts, and garbage. Shell fragments from dropping mussel shells onto rocks from high in the air.

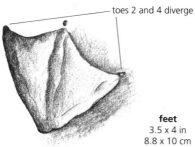

toes 2 and 4 diverge

feet
3.5 x 4 in
8.8 x 10 cm

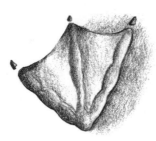

walk

TRACK LENGTH

TRACK WIDTH

Eagles
various species

Large birds, averaging
35 in (90 cm) in length,
with wingspans of 80 in
(200 cm). Brown
bodies. Adult golden
eagle (*Aquila
chrysaetos*) has golden
feathers over head and neck.
Adult bald eagle (*Haliaeetus leucocephalus*) has
white head, neck, and tail feathers.

Bald eagle
Haliaeetus leucocephalus

Track: Four wide, robust toes. Toes
2–4 point forward. Lacks webbing
and metatarsal pad. Claws are long,
sharp, and not attached to the toe
print.

Trail: Walking stride about 18 in (45
cm). Golden eagle will run after prey
on the ground.

Scat: Semiliquid, primarily white with
some brown intermixed.

Habitat: Golden eagle found in mountainous areas and hunts
over open country. Bald eagle usually found near lakes and
rivers.

cough pellet

**urine stain
on rock**

Similar species: Larger than hawk's track, which is less than 3 in (7.5 cm). Differ from owls by having three toes pointing forward. Differ from geese and swans by lacking webbing. Differ from herons and cranes by having symmetrical feet.

Other sign: Cough pellets may be 5 x 1.5 in (12.5 x 3.8 cm). Nests may be 6 ft (2 m) in diameter.

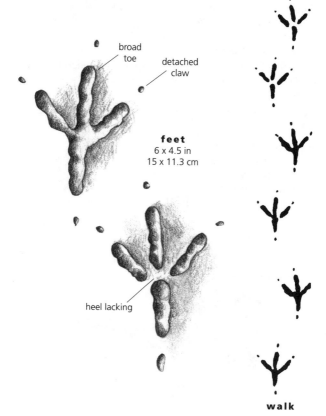

broad toe

detached claw

feet
6 x 4.5 in
15 x 11.3 cm

heel lacking

walk

Blue Grouse
Dendragapus obscurus

Size comparable to a chicken, averaging 18 in (45 cm). Male is speckled gray, black, and white, with yellow eye combs and dark throat. Females are uniformly mottled brown.

Track: Four toes, with toes 2–4 pointing forward. Toe 1, relatively short, may not show. Toes are relatively wide and lack webbing. Feet point forward to slightly inward. In a clear print, a narrow fringe of scales may show around toes. In winter, feathers on feet show.

Trail: Walking stride is about 9.5 in (24 cm).

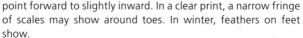

Scat: Light to dark brown, sometimes with white nitrogenous covering. Content includes buds, berries, and sawdust. In winter, scat accumulates in large mass of 50 or so in snow nest.

scat
1.5 x 0.25 in
3.8 x 0.6 cm

Habitat: Coniferous forest to the upper timberline.

Similar species: Differ from other forest birds by wide, robust toe size and short toe 1. Short stride and wide straddle of grouse trail different than other forest bird trails.

Other sign: Fly into or burrow under the snow to roost. Tunnel to nest makes a sharp turn, perhaps to confuse predators.

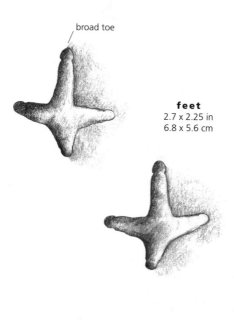

broad toe

feet
2.7 x 2.25 in
6.8 x 5.6 cm

walk

TRACK LENGTH

TRACK WIDTH

Scaled Quail
Callipepla squamata

Small, chicken-like bird, averaging 10 in (25 cm). Gray back with brownish wings. White crest on head. Chest is scaled by black-edged feathers.

Track: Four toes. Toes 2–4 point forward and slightly outward. Toes 3 and 4 nearly equal in length. Toe 1 detached, but usually registers. Toes relatively wide; lack webbing. Claws attached.

Trail: Walking stride 8–10 in (20–25 cm). Feet point slightly inward.

Scat: Long, thin cord, light to dark brown, occasionally with white nitrogenous covering. Diet of dry vegetation causes scat texture to resemble sawdust. When dry, may break into small fragments.

scat
up to 0.6 x 0.1 in
up to 1.5 x 0.3 cm

ground roost

SCAT WIDTH

Habitat: Arid grasslands, plains, and open shrubland. Wide range includes several species of quail.

Similar species: Differs from grouse by having less robust tracks, narrower toes, and toe 2's tending to be shorter than toes 3 and 4. Tracks are clearer than grouse, especially in winter, as quail lacks toe feathers. Toes broader than those of other ground-dwelling birds. Lack of webbing separates tracks from aquatic birds.

Other sign: Look for dust bath depressions along trails. Ground roosts form a circle of depressions where each bird's tail points into center.

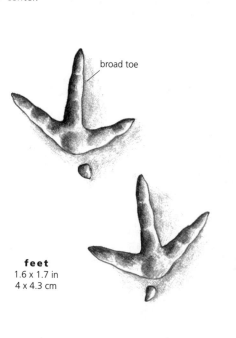

broad toe

feet
1.6 x 1.7 in
4 x 4.3 cm

walk

TRACK LENGTH

TRACK WIDTH

Turkey
Meleagris gallopavo

Large, ground-dwelling bird. Males average 45 in (113 cm) and females 35 in (88 cm) in length. Smaller and more slender than the domesticated "Thanksgiving" turkey. Male has a dark brown to black body, with white stripes on flight feather; tail feathers are tipped with brownish white. Color of female's feathers is similar but dull. Male also has red *wattles*, folds of skin hanging from the chin.

Track: Four broad, robust toes. Toes 2–4 face forward. Hind toe (toe 1) only occasionally registers, and then in a straight line with toe 4. Only the claw or tip of toe 1 registers. Metatarsal pad present, though it may be unattached to toes. Claws narrow and usually attached to toe.

Trail: Walking stride 15 in (38 cm). Foot axis may vary, pointing into the line of travel or turning slightly out.

scat
3 x 0.5 in
7.5 x 1.3 cm

tracks with scratch marks

SCAT WIDTH

Scat: Solid scat is long, up to 3 in (7.5 cm), narrow, and brown with greenish white nitrogenous material on ends. Also produces a soft scat that piles in a shapeless mass on ground.

Habitat: Open forest and shrubland, in trees with lateral branches for roosting at night.

Similar species: Differs from other birds by wide, robust toes. Tracks larger than other ground-dwelling birds. Lacks webbing of ducks and certain other aquatic birds. Separated from eagles by presence (usually) of metatarsal pad. Toes 2 and 4 point forward to a greater degree than those of crane.

Other sign: Scratches on ground where turkey digs for seeds, acorns, nuts, and insects.

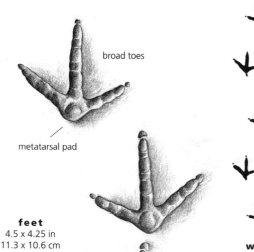

broad toes

metatarsal pad

feet
4.5 x 4.25 in
11.3 x 10.6 cm

walk

TRACK LENGTH

HALF TRACK WIDTH

Owls
various species

Considerable variation in length, from the saw-whet owl *(Aegolius acadicus)*, 8 in (20 cm), to the short-eared owl *(Asio flammeus)*, 15 in (38 cm), to the great gray owl *(Strix nebulosa)*, 25 in (63 cm). All species have immobile eyes offset by facial disks of feathers. Great variability in appearance between species. Typical body colors are grays, browns, and reddish browns.

Short-eared owl
Asio flammeus

Track: Four broad toes, with two paired and facing forward. Toe 4 position is not fixed and may face back or out. Lack webbing and metatarsal pads. Claws long and detached from footprint. Tracks of great horned owl *(Bubo virginianus)* illustrated.

Trail: Walking stride varies considerably among species, from 3 in (7.5 cm) to 10 in (25 cm).

cough pellet

perch branch

cough pellets

perch with pellets

Scat: Semiliquid, primarily white.

Habitat: Forested areas. Some species, such as barn owls, will readily use human structures.

Similar species: Differ from most birds in toes 2 and 3 being paired, nearly parallel, and pointing forward. Differ from woodpeckers by toes being wide and robust, and by toes 1 and 4 being much shorter than toes 2 and 3.

Other sign: Cough pellets below a roost. Diameter of cough pellets ranges from 0.25–1 in (0.6–2.5 cm) and is directly related to the size of the owl. Pellets are shiny and black when new but turn gray with age.

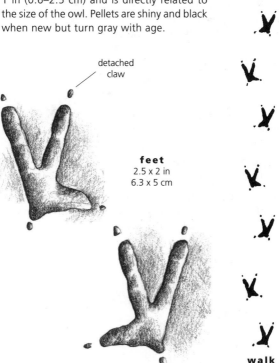

detached claw

feet
2.5 x 2 in
6.3 x 5 cm

walk

TRACK LENGTH

TRACK WIDTH

Northern Flicker
Colaptes auratus

Medium-sized woodpecker, slightly larger than the American robin, average length 12 in (30 cm). Male has brown-barred back, black chest, white rump, red or black whisker stripe, and red or orange under wings. Female lacks whisker stripe.

Track: Four toes, with two parallel and pointing forward. Toes 1 and 4 point backward and are not equal in length. Strong, rigid tail feathers may show on ground.

Trail: Walking stride is about 3 in (7.5 cm). Hopping stride is about 4 in (10 cm).

Scat: Cord, about four times longer than wide. Often contains undigested parts of insects.

Habitat: Open woodlands, cottonwood bottoms, and around towns.

Similar species: Differs from three-toed woodpecker by presence of toe 1. Differs from other birds its size by having two toes pointing forward.

scat
1 x .25 in
2.5 x 0.6 cm

SCAT WIDTH

Other sign: Excavates and nests in tree cavities. Does not add bedding material to cavity nest.

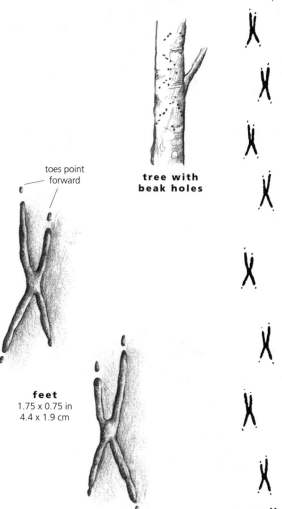

tree with beak holes

toes point forward

feet
1.75 x 0.75 in
4.4 x 1.9 cm

walk

Black-billed Magpie

Pica pica

Black and iridescent-green body, wings, and unusually long tail. White belly and black beak. Average length about 20 in (50 cm).

Track: Four medium-wide toes, three facing forward. Toe 1 nearly as long as toes 2, 3, and 4. Lacks webbing and metatarsal pad. Claws long and detached from footprint.

Trail: Walking stride is about 6 in (15 cm).

Scat: Semiliquid, brown with white intermixed.

cough pellet

Habitat: Lower mountains, in open woodlands, thickets, along stream edges. Often found near human habitation.

Similar species: Differs from songbirds by larger size and relatively wide toes. Smaller than crows and ravens.

Other sign: Caches food in trees and under bark. Cough pellet is 1.25 x 0.4 in (3.1 x 1 cm).

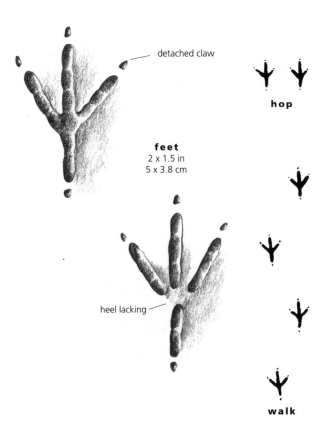

detached claw

feet
2 x 1.5 in
5 x 3.8 cm

heel lacking

hop

walk

TRACK LENGTH

TRACK WIDTH

Crow
Corvus brachyrhynchos

Medium (17 in / 43 cm) black bird with strong beak (smaller than raven's). Sides of tail are parallel in flight, not wedge shaped. Black feet and legs.

Track: Four toes, three facing forward. Toe 1 nearly equals toes 2, 3, and 4. Lacks webbing. Metatarsal pad present. Claws long and often detached from footprint. The footprint length of 2.5 in (6.3 cm) includes toe 4 which adds 0.7 in (1.8 cm).

Trail: Walking stride varies but is about 5 in (13 cm). Crows both walk and hop and may run with a long stride.

Scat: Semiliquid brown and white, but may contain remnants of food from their omnivorous diet.

cough pellet

Habitat: Roadsides, woodlands, farms, orchards, and lake and ocean shores; found near water in southwest during winter.

Similar species: Raven track and trail is much larger than crow's. Lack the paired forward facing toes of owls. Lack long toe 1 of hawks.

Other sign: Cough pellets up to 1 x 0.4 in (2.5 x 1.0 cm). Pellets may contain berries, seeds, nuts, insect parts, and snails, among other items of its varied diet.

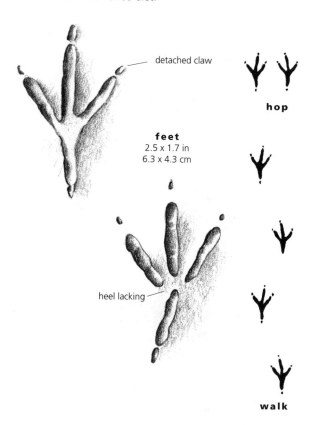

detached claw

hop

feet
2.5 x 1.7 in
6.3 x 4.3 cm

heel lacking

walk

TRACK LENGTH

TRACK WIDTH

Common Raven
Corvus corax

Large black bird, average length 24 in (60 cm). Beak heavy. Tail is wedge shaped in flight. Size varies considerably, though male is larger than female.

Track: Four toes, toes 2–4 facing forward. Length of toe 1 nearly equals toes 2, 3, and 4. Lacks webbing and metatarsal pad. Claws long and detached from footprint.

Trail: Walking stride varies considerably, but is about 20 in (50 cm). Also runs, with a longer stride.

Scat: Semiliquid, brown, black, and white. Often oily. May contain remnants of its omnivorous diet.

Habitat: Mountains, especially where carcasses of deer and elk can be found, and at garbage dumps. Will beg food from picnickers.

cough pellet

Similar species: Track and trail of the common crow are diminutive versions of the raven's. Lacks the paired forward facing toes of owls. Lacks the long toe 1 of hawks. Smaller than eagle's.

Other sign: Cough pellets up to 3 x 0.5 in (7.5 x 1.3 cm). Caches food in forks of trees and, often by burying.

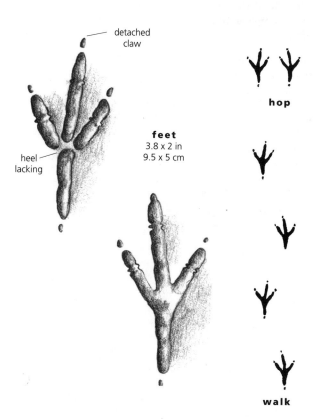

detached claw

heel lacking

feet
3.8 x 2 in
9.5 x 5 cm

hop

walk

Roadrunner
Geococcyx californianus

Medium-sized, ground-dwelling cuckoo, averaging 23 in (60 cm), who runs rapidly and seldom flies. Brown and white-streaked body with a dark crest. Long tail, tipped with white.

Track: Four relatively long, slender toes. Toes 1 and 4 point backward. Toes 1 and 4 similar in length to toes 2 and 3. Claws on toes 2 and 3 detached and prominent. Claws on toes 1 and 4 usually do not register.

Trail: Running stride averages 16 in (40 cm), but may be considerably longer as the roadrunner can leave the ground in midstride.

Scat: No record.

Habitat: Shrub desert including mesquite and chaparral.

Similar species: Four toes, with two pointing forward includes ospreys, owls, cuckoos, kingfishers, and four-toed woodpeckers. Woodpecker track distinct in that toes 1 and 4 are not similar in length to toes 2 and 3. Toes 2 and 3 of the kingfisher are closely joined by webbing. Osprey and owl tracks have broader, more robust toes. Habitat is a good clue to identification.

Other sign: Nest in low thicket or cactus may contain snake skins and mammal feces.

feet
2.4 x 1.4 in
6 x 3.4 cm

walk

TRACK LENGTH

TRACK WIDTH

Opossum

Didelphis virginiana

The size of a large
domestic cat, but
more stout,
nearly hairless,
and with a
round, rat-like tail.
Weight from 8–14 lb
(3.5–6.5 kg). Face whitish,
with thin, black-edged ears.
Body is whitish with gray and black
hairs interspersed.

Track: Five toes. Distinct hind print with an opposable (like the human thumb) inside toe protruding side-ways from other toes. Outside toe is slightly separated from middle three toes. Front footprint is wider than long and shows long toes that widen slightly toward the end.

Trail: Walking stride 18 in (45 cm). Walking trail often reflects slow movement, with hind footprint registering behind the front. Trail is sloppy and footprints sel-dom register directly. Tail drag often shows. Walking pattern

scat shape is highly variable

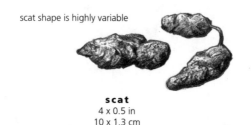

scat
4 x 0.5 in
10 x 1.3 cm

SCAT WIDTH

occasionally similar to raccoon's, where the hind footprint registers beside the front footprint.

Scat: Highly variable shape and size and lack of distinctive form reflect highly variable, omnivorous diet. Single scat up to 4 in (10 cm) long.

Habitat: Prefers riparian areas, woodlands, and farmyards. Habitat not restricted by diet, as the opossum will eat small mammals, birds, eggs, reptiles, amphibians, fish, carrion, fruit, and any garbage it can find.

Similar species: Trail may be confused with those of muskrats, woodrats, and domestic rats when a tail drag is present. However, the distinctive hind footprint and large size of the opossum identify its trail.

Other sign: Dens in logs, stumps, rock crevices, and dens of other animals.

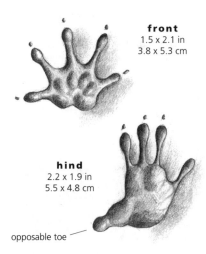

front
1.5 x 2.1 in
3.8 x 5.3 cm

hind
2.2 x 1.9 in
5.5 x 4.8 cm

opposable toe

walk

FRONT TRACK LENGTH

FRONT TRACK WIDTH

Shrews
various species

Smaller than mice, less than 0.25 oz (7 g). Long, pointed nose. Minute eyes and ears. Color brown to black, with gray to white belly. Eats mostly insects.

Wandering shrew
Sorex vagrans

Track: Five slender toes present on front and hind feet. In clear prints, four interdigital and two proximal pads may be seen.

Trail: Hopping stride seldom more than 2 in (5 cm). The group of tracks is less than 1 in (2.5 cm) long. Seldom is the stride more than three times the group.

Scat: Usually small pellets with tapered ends.

Habitat: Found everywhere from deserts to alpine areas. Look for tracks in wet, fine mud of riparian areas or in snow along logs or building edges. Wood piles and leaf litter make good homes. Wide range includes several species of shrews.

——— tapered ends

scat
0.2 x 0.1 in
0.5 x 0.3 cm

insect remains

Similar species: Differ from mice and voles by having five toes on front foot.

Other sign: After eating, leave body parts from insects they have killed. Often burrow just below the surface of the snow, opening tunnels that partially collapse and expose their route. Trails in the snow radiate from holes like spokes of a wheel.

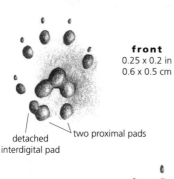

front
0.25 x 0.2 in
0.6 x 0.5 cm

detached interdigital pad

two proximal pads

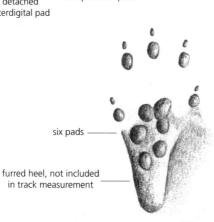

six pads

furred heel, not included in track measurement

hind
0.3 x 0.2 in
0.8 x 0.5 cm

bound

FRONT TRACK LENGTH

FRONT TRACK WIDTH

Armadillo

Dasypus novemcinctus

Size of a house cat, weighing 8–17 lb (3.5–8 kg). Body, tail, and head are covered with a horny "armor" derived from the leathery skin. A few hairs are found between scales. Body color a light tan to gray. Large gray to black ears.

Track: Front tracks with four toes, hind with five. Often only the prominent inner toes, two on front, 3 on rear, register. Claws are prominent and broad, may appear attached, and usually dig deeply into the ground.

sign

scat
2 x 0.4 in
5 x 1 cm

SCAT WIDTH

Trail: Trotting stride is about 25 in (65 cm), walking stride around 15 in (40 cm). Use side gaits including trots and lopes. Occasionally the belly or tail drags.

Scat: Usually elongate, but may be spherical. Usually contains insect remains and a considerable amount of dirt.

Habitat: Usually dry, sandy areas including brush, woodlands, and chaparral. Seem to additionally prefer rocky areas and cliffs.

Similar species: Easily separated from other mammals by prominent claws and odd numbers of toes in tracks.

Other sign: Digs out ant mounds and disturbs ground litter as it roots for insects. Digs long dwelling burrows that are around 8 in (20 cm) in diameter. Pulls vegetation into the burrows to form a nest.

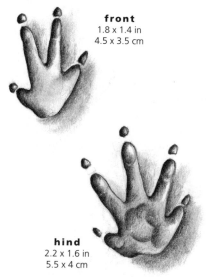

front
1.8 x 1.4 in
4.5 x 3.5 cm

hind
2.2 x 1.6 in
5.5 x 4 cm

walk

FRONT TRACK LENGTH

FRONT TRACK WIDTH

Red Fox
Vulpes vulpes

Border collie–sized, 6–15 lb (3–7 kg). Reddish yellow, with black stockings and a white tip on the tail.
Regional color phases include silver, black, and bluish gray. Long, pointed ears and elongate, pointed muzzle.

Track: Claws prominent. A ridge of callus present across interdigital pad. One lobe on the leading edge of the interdigital pad. Inside toe slightly larger than outside. Front foot larger than hind.

Trail: Trotting stride averages 32 in (80 cm). Typically uses a trotting gait and, occasionally, a 2 x 2 trot with body turned to the side. Walks more than coyote, especially in shrubs.

Scat: Often has tapered tail. Composition varies. Mouse or rabbit fur, berries, and insects are common. Bird feathers and plant remains often present.

Habitat: Found in a variety of habitats from brush to croplands to mixed hard- and softwood forest. Prefers edges, where hunt-

scat
2 x 0.6 in
5 x 1.5 cm

log

SCAT WIDTH

ing for small mammals is good. Also found in urban areas, where cover is available during the daytime. Not found in dense forests.

Similar species: Differs from other canids by having a ridge of callus on the interdigital pad. Track tends to be larger than gray fox and usually shows claws. Differs from bobcat in having only one lobe on the interdigital pad and claws (usually) showing.

Other sign: Multiple dens are used each season. Often digs own den. A given den may be used for several years. Look for small bones around den entrance. Scat has a diagnostic musky odor, produced by a musk gland on the top of the tail. Learn to identify this unique "foxy" odor. Foxes tightrope-walk on narrow logs.

side trot

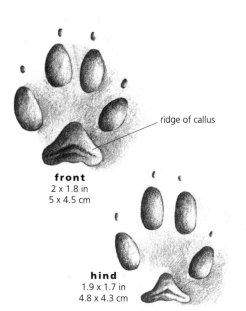

ridge of callus

front
2 x 1.8 in
5 x 4.5 cm

hind
1.9 x 1.7 in
4.8 x 4.3 cm

trot

FRONT TRACK LENGTH

FRONT TRACK WIDTH

Gray Fox
Urocyon cinereoargenteus

Smaller than a border collie, 8–11 lb (4–5 kg). Body color is pepper-and-salt. A black stripe runs down the back and upper side of tail. Sides are reddish. Tip of tail is black. Long, pointed ears and elongate, pointed muzzle.

Track: Small for a canid, somewhat broad and therefore somewhat cat-like. Claws, rarely present in track, are very small and sharp, giving the gray fox the ability to climb trees like a cat. Front foot larger than hind.

Trail: Generally a trot. Trotting stride averages 24 in (60 cm). Walks more than coyote.

Scat: Often has tapered tail. Composition varies, as the gray fox is opportunistic when feeding. Rabbit fur is most common, followed by fur of other small mammals, berries, and insects. Plant remains are often present.

scat
2 x 0.6 in
5 x 1.5 cm

SCAT WIDTH

Habitat: Prefers a mixture of fields, early-stage woodlands, and riparian areas. More common in woodlands than red fox.

Similar species: Smaller than coyote and wolf. Lacks the ridge of callus on the interdigital pad of the red fox. Differs from coyote in that claws often do not show.

Other sign: Seldom digs dens, but uses woodpiles, rock outcrops, hollow trees, and brushpiles. Look for small bones around den entrances.

side trot

climbing tree

— no callus ridge

front
1.8 x 1.6 in
4.5 x 4 cm

hind
1.7 x 1.6 in
4.3 x 4 cm

trot

FRONT TRACK LENGTH

FRONT TRACK WIDTH

Kit Fox
Vulpes macrotis

The size of a domestic cat, 3–5 lb (1.4–2.3 kg), with disproportionately large ears. Body color is pale red washed with gray. Tail has a black tip. Swift fox (*Vulpes velox*), a closely related species, is found in the northeast part of the region covered here.

Track: Small for a canid. Claws often do not show. Front foot larger than hind.

Trail: Walking stride 14 in (35 cm). Loping stride 22 in (55 cm). Dainty trail often mistaken for that of a cat. Details of footprint seldom register in sand.

Scat: Usually has a tapered tail. Scat consists mostly of small mammals and insects, but occasionally birds and reptiles.

scat
2 x 0.6 in
5 x 1.5 cm

SCAT WIDTH

Habitat: Found in sand habitats of the desert or plains where vegetation is sparse and short.

Similar species: Smaller than coyote, whose claws show better. Lacks the ridge of callus on the interdigital pad of the red fox. Tracks may be smaller than gray fox, although distinction may be difficult, but the sand habitat is a good clue.

Other sign: Dens in burrows in the ground, where it hides during the day.

lope

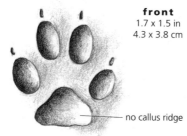

front
1.7 x 1.5 in
4.3 x 3.8 cm

— no callus ridge

hind
1.3 x 1.2 in
3.3 x 3 cm

walk

FRONT TRACK LENGTH

FRONT TRACK WIDTH

Coyote
Canis latrans

Collie-sized canid, 20–25 lb (9–11 kg). Male larger than female. Color varies from completely gray to tan to rust. Long, pointed ears and long, narrow muzzle.

Track: Claws usually present. One lobe on the leading edge of the interdigital pad. Inside toe slightly larger than outside. Front foot larger than hind.

Trail: Trotting stride averages 39 in (98 cm). Often trots with body turned to the side, leaving a 2 x 2 track. Often lopes, leaving a C-shaped pattern.

Scat: Varies from pure black animal protein to mostly hair with some bones. Tips tapered into long tails.

Habitat: An animal of the open brush country, the coyote digs its den on exposed hilltops or ridges with a view of surrounding area. Where trapped and hunted, may den in a more secluded location.

Similar species: Even adult track is smaller than that of a wolf pup. Track may overlap in size with red fox, but lacks callus

scat
3 x 0.6 in
7.5 x 1.5 cm

SCAT WIDTH

ridge of red fox. Track larger than gray fox, and usually shows claws. Differs from bobcat by showing claws and by having one lobe on leading edge of interdigital pad.

Other sign: Marks territory with urine and scat piles. Scat pile locations may be used repeatedly. Uses feet to scratch near scat piles, spreading odor from scat and foot.

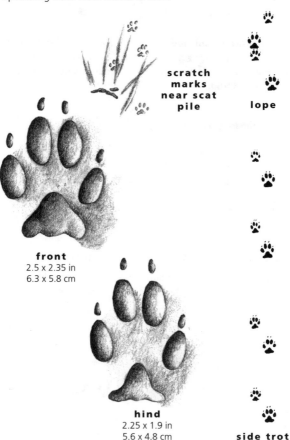

scratch
marks
near scat
pile

lope

front
2.5 x 2.35 in
6.3 x 5.8 cm

hind
2.25 x 1.9 in
5.6 x 4.8 cm

side trot

Jaguarundi
Felis yagouaroundi

Slightly larger than a house cat, 10–20 lb (4.5–9 kg). Elongate shape, long tail, and short legs earned the name weasel cat. Ears are short, round, and widely set. Head is broad and flat. Two unspotted homogeneous color phases may exist in one litter—blackish to brownish gray or reddish yellow. Very rare in the United States.

Track: Front tracks are round or wider than long. Hind tracks longer than wide. Claw impressions are usually absent. Toes form a distinct arc and toe 3 leads. The leading edge of the interdigital pad has two lobes. Inside toe distinctly larger than outside toe. Like the track of a large house cat. Measurements from two animals (one each Mexico and Texas) and literature.

Trail: Walking stride is about 13 in (33 cm). Little else known.

Scat: No records, but probably typical of cat family. Uniform diameter cord with slight constrictions; ends usually blunt. When

broken
constriction

scat
3.6 x 0.4 in
9 x 1 cm

SCAT WIDTH

feeding on a dry diet, scat constricts and falls apart in short segments.

Habitat: Dense cover including thorny acacia and mesquite chaparral, and dry deciduous forests including scrub oak and sable palm.

Similar species: Cannot be definitively separated from a house cat. Smaller than other North American cats. Differ from those of fox by presence of two lobes on the anterior edge of the interdigital pad.

Other sign: None reported.

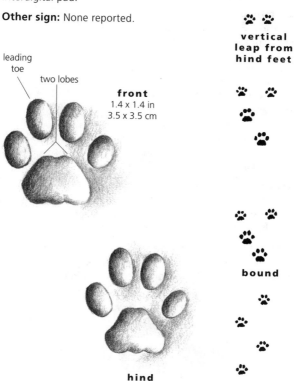

walk

vertical
leap from
hind feet

bound

walk

leading
toe

two lobes

front
1.4 x 1.4 in
3.5 x 3.5 cm

hind
1.1 x 1 in
2.7 x 2.6 cm

Bobcat
Felis rufus

Collie-sized, with male averaging 17 lb (8 kg) and female 13 lb (6 kg). Overall color reddish to yellowish brown, with dark spots or streaks and whitish underside. Ears have tufts at tips. Back of ears and top of tail tip black. Tail is short or "bobbed," about 4 in (10 cm) long.

Track: Front track is round or wider than long. Hind track may be longer than wide. Claw impressions are usually absent. Toes form a slight arc and toe 3 leads. The leading edge of the interdigital pad has two lobes. Inside toe distinctly larger than outside toe.

Trail: Walking stride is about 20 in (50 cm). Usually walks, but bounds with hind feet placed side by side when chasing prey. Winter trails often show random vertical leaps, perhaps signalling that the bobcat has jumped after a flying bird.

Scat: Tends to be constricted and, if dry, separates at constrictions into segments. Ends usually blunt. Dry scat falls apart. Scat from a fresh kill may form a cord of uniform diameter.

broken constriction

scat
3 x 0.8 in
7.5 x 2 cm

SCAT WIDTH

Habitat: Prefers dense cover of swamps and forests, especially with rocky ledges. Open agricultural land is not used. Rock piles, caves, and high rocky ledges are important for bearing young.

Similar species: Differs from coyote by lacking claws, having two lobes on the leading edge of the interdigital pad, and having toe 3 leading. Substantially smaller than both lion and lynx.

Other sign: Scent marks made by urine, scat, and anal glands. Scrapes dirt or snow over urine and scat, and scratches from rubbing glands are apparent on snow; claw marks on trees. Caches food by burying.

walk

vertical leap from hind feet

claw marks on tree

bound

walk

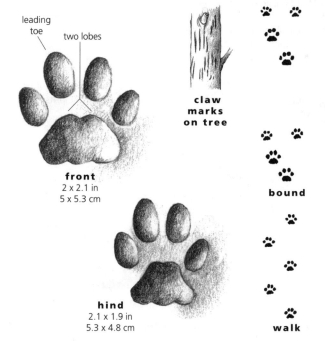

leading toe

two lobes

front
2 x 2.1 in
5 x 5.3 cm

hind
2.1 x 1.9 in
5.3 x 4.8 cm

FRONT TRACK LENGTH

FRONT TRACK WIDTH

Ocelot
Felis pardalis

Collie-sized,
weighing up to
35 lb (16 kg).
More slender than a
bobcat. Body color is
gray, buff, or
cinnamon with black-
rimmed, brown
markings ranging in
shape from spots on body to stripes
on neck. Underside white with
black markings. Long tail marked
with black stripes or rings.

Track: Appears long for cats, with
hind tracks much longer than wide.
Claw impressions are usually absent.
Toes form a distinct arc and toe 3
leads. The leading edge of the interdigital pad has two lobes.
Inside toe distinctly larger than outside toe. Measurements from
five ocelots from Texas.

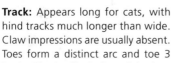

sign

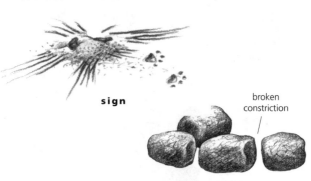

broken
constriction

scat
3 x 0.8 in
7.5 x 2 cm

Trail: Trotting stride is about 40 in (100 cm).

Scat: Tends to be constricted and, if dry, separates at constrictions into segments. Dry scat falls apart. Ends usually blunt. Scat from a fresh kill may form a uniform-diameter cord. Defecate at latrines, where feces accumulate.

Habitat: Seldom far from trees or dense cover. In Texas, found in dense, thorny chaparral of mesquite and acacia.

Similar species: Smaller than jaguar and lion, and larger than jaguarundi. Definitive characteristics are not available to separate ocelot tracks from bobcat. However, tracks are probably longer. Differ from those of fox by presence of two lobes on the anterior edge of the interdigital pad.

Other sign: Probably scent marks with urine and scat. Scrapes dirt over scat. Scratches trees and fence posts.

walk

vertical
leap from
hind feet

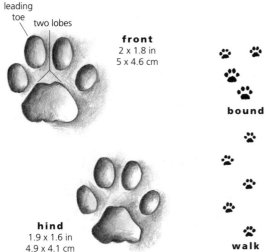

leading
toe two lobes

front
2 x 1.8 in
5 x 4.6 cm

hind
1.9 x 1.6 in
4.9 x 4.1 cm

bound

walk

FRONT TRACK LENGTH

FRONT TRACK WIDTH

Mountain Lion
Puma concolor

Larger than a German shepherd, with male averaging 145 lb (66 kg) and female about 120 lb (54 kg). Color  **gray to red, often called tawny, with whitish underside. Back of ears and tip of tail black to brown. Tail is more than half the length of the body. Also called cougar or puma.**

Track: Track diameter of a baseball. Front track round or wider than long, and hind track longer than wide. Claw impressions are usually absent. Toes form a slight arc and toe 3 leads. Leading edge of the interdigital pad has two lobes. Inside toe distinctly larger.

Trail: Walking stride is about 36 in (90 cm). Usually walks, but bounds when chasing prey.

Scat: Scat from a fresh kill may form a cord of uniform diameter with very slight constrictions; ends usually blunt. As the carcass a lion is feeding on dries out, the lion's scat tends to develop constrictions, eventually falling apart when diet becomes very dry.

scat
4 x 1.25 in
10 x 3.1 cm

Habitat: Habitat is that of its main prey, deer. Open woodlands with rock ledges and grass (for deer) preferred. Often found in riparian zones with trees.

Similar species: Track differs from canids by the presence of two lobes on the leading edge of the interdigital pad, by having toe 3 leading, and by usually not showing claws.

Other sign: Often buries scat by scraping dirt over it with front feet. Scraped ground material may conceal food caches. Male will rake up basketball-sized patches of brush and urinate on them to mark home range.

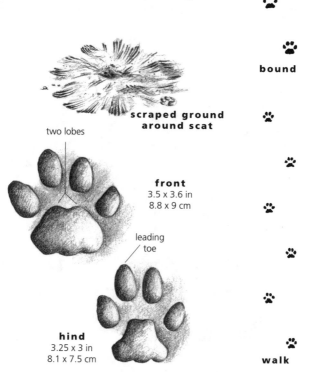

scraped ground around scat

two lobes

front
3.5 x 3.6 in
8.8 x 9 cm

leading toe

hind
3.25 x 3 in
8.1 x 7.5 cm

bound

walk

FRONT TRACK LENGTH

FRONT TRACK WIDTH

Jaguar
Panthera onca

Larger than a
Doberman
pincher, with
weights usually
between 110–260 lb
(50–120 kg). Total
length with tail may
reach 8 ft (2.4 m).
Skull appears large on body. Largest of North American cats.
Females about 10 percent smaller. Color is buff to light gold
with black rosettes; black jaguars do exist. Extremely rare in
the United States.

Track: Track larger than a softball.
Front tracks round or wider than
long, and hind tracks slightly longer
than wide. Toes form a slight arc and
toe 3 leads. Leading edge of the
interdigital pad has two lobes. Toes
more rounded. Inside toe distinctly
larger. Measurements are from two
jaguars from Venezuela.

Trail: Walking stride is 40–55 in (100–140 cm).

Scat: Uniform diameter cord with slight constrictions; ends usually
blunt. When feeding on a dry diet, scat constricts and falls apart
in short segments.

scat
6.4 x 1.5 in
16 x 3.8 cm

Habitat: In the United States found in dry, hilly country with rock outcroppings or cliffs interspersed with pinyon pine–juniper vegetation. This may represent a marginal habitat limiting northern extension of range.

Similar species: Track differs from mountain lion by having more broad, rounded tips on toes and its massive size. Tracks larger than all other felid species. Differ from those of canids by presence of two lobes on the anterior edge of the interdigital pad.

Other sign: Probably makes circular scrapes to mark by urination and probably covers scat in a similar manner to other felids.

bound

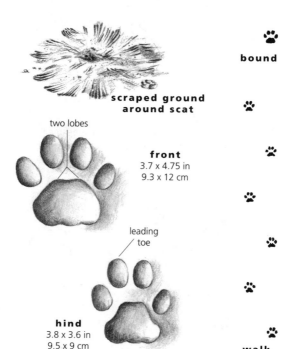

scraped ground
around scat

two lobes

front
3.7 x 4.75 in
9.3 x 12 cm

leading
toe

hind
3.8 x 3.6 in
9.5 x 9 cm

walk

FRONT TRACK LENGTH

HALF FRONT TRACK WIDTH

Black Bear
Ursus americanus

Calf-sized bear, female averaging 120 lb (54 kg) and male about 300 lb (135 kg). Male grows faster and obtains larger size than female. **Color varies from black to brown to blond to red.**

Track: Claws on front foot, seldom longer than toes, are usually present. Little toe is set back from rest of toes. Hind print has a large, humanlike heel. Outside toe is larger than others.

Trail: Walking stride 35–40 in (88–100 cm). Usually ambles, a fast walk where the hind foot oversteps the front. Gait is pigeon-toed. Lopes in a C-shaped pattern or a side gallop.

Scat: Normally contains vegetation and is sweet smelling. When feeding on carcasses, scat varies from black to brown, with mostly

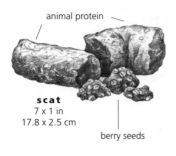

animal protein

scat
7 x 1 in
17.8 x 2.5 cm

berry seeds

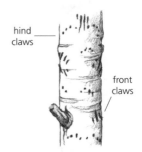

hind claws

front claws

claw marks on tree

hair and some bones. Ants often found in scat. Tips have a short taper or are blunt.

Habitat: Forest, seldom venturing far into wide openings. Thick understory vegetation and abundant food sources are critical.

Similar species: Differs from grizzly bear by smaller size, shorter claw length, and more curved arc of toes. Differs from lion and wolf by having five toes.

Other sign: Claws trees, rips open logs, digs into ant piles, and turns over rocks and scat as it looks for insects, but seldom digs out roots.

side lope

lope

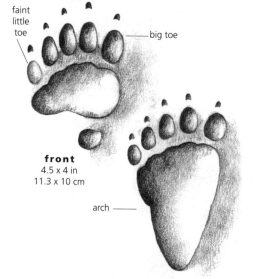

faint little toe

big toe

front
4.5 x 4 in
11.3 x 10 cm

arch

hind
7 x 3.5 in
17.8 x 8.8 cm

amble

FRONT TRACK LENGTH

FRONT TRACK WIDTH

Ringtail
Bassariscus astutus

Small, rat-sized, with a bushy tail as long as its body. Males average 1.5–2.5 lb (0.7–1.1 kg), with females slightly smaller. Pointed face, large eyes and ears. Tan to gray overall, with some black hairs. Tail has black bands alternating with white to a black tip.

Track: Five toes, round and somewhat bulbous, with an extra proximal pad showing in the front print. Claws are semi-retractile and may not show.

Trail: Bounding stride is 12–16 in (30–40 cm). Uses a relatively slow bound or lope much of the time.

Scat: Usually composed of plant material, but occasionally black animal protein scats are found. Insects and fruits are often present.

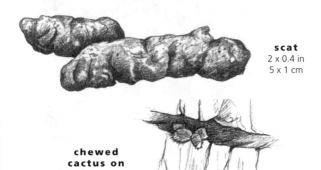

scat
2 x 0.4 in
5 x 1 cm

chewed cactus on cliff runway

SCAT WIDTH

Habitat: Found in a variety of habitats from riparian to desert to open woodland to evergreen forest. Rest sites and dens are located in rocks, burrows, brushpiles, and hollow limbs. Not averse to using buildings for nests and dens.

Similar species: Differs from domestic cats, bobcats, and small foxes by having five toes and an extra proximal pad.

Other sign: Runways at the bases of cliffs are used repeatedly, and trails often lead to a single rock crevice where it dens.

lope

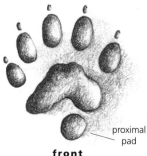

proximal pad

front
1 x 1 in
2.5 x 2.5 cm

hind
1 x 1 in
2.5 x 2.5 cm

bound

FRONT TRACK LENGTH

FRONT TRACK WIDTH

Raccoon
Procyon lotor

Stocky, smaller
than a collie, with
broad head and
bushy tail. Male
averages 18 lb (8 kg)
and female 16 lb
(7 kg). Gray to black overall, with black rings on the tail and a
black mask on a white face.

Track: Five slender toes, slightly bulbous on the ends. Feet resemble small
human hands and feet. Hind foot has
a long, naked heel.

Trail: Walking stride averages 27 in
(68 cm). Roll of hips during walk
causes hind foot to register beside
the opposite front print. C-shaped
gallop is common.

Scat: Highly variable, but often black, even-diameter cord with
blunt ends. Often contains crayfish or fruit. Deposited singly or
in dung heaps containing scat from perhaps several individuals.
May carry a parasite fatal to humans. Do not smell scat,
and wash hands after touching.

Habitat: River and stream drainages are prime habitats, but
storm drains in cities may also provide refuge.

blunt end /

scat
3 x 0.75 in
7.5 x 1.9 cm

SCAT WIDTH

Similar species: Differs from bear in having slender toes. Differs from both river otter and mink by lack of webbing. Larger than mink.

Other sign: Digs holes in stream banks for crayfish. Leaves piles of crayfish skeletons and claws. Digs for worms in lawns.

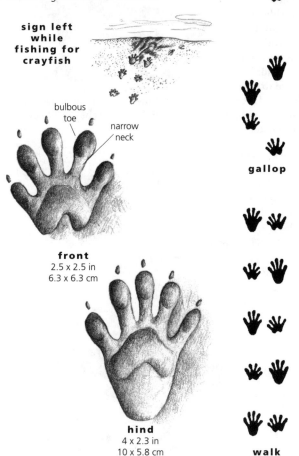

sign left while fishing for crayfish

bulbous toe

narrow neck

front
2.5 x 2.5 in
6.3 x 6.3 cm

hind
4 x 2.3 in
10 x 5.8 cm

gallop

walk

FRONT TRACK LENGTH

FRONT TRACK WIDTH

Coati
Nasua narica

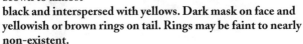

Larger than a collie, weighing 15–25 lb (7–11 kg). Distinguished by their long tail and long snout. Considerable body color variation ranging from pale reddish brown to almost black and interspersed with yellows. Dark mask on face and yellowish or brown rings on tail. Rings may be faint to nearly non-existent.

Track: Five toes on front and hind tracks. Toes are slightly bulbous at tips. Hind track shows a long, naked heel that may not register on a hard surface. Claw length equals or exceeds toe length.

Trail: Walking stride is 14 in (36 cm). Generally a rambling trail investigating many objects.

scat
2.8 x 0.6 in
7 x 1.5 cm

SCAT WIDTH

Scat: Highly variable depending on the diet. Often a black, even-diameter cord with blunt ends.

Habitat: Prefers chaparral to open dry deciduous forests.

Similar species: Differs from raccoon by presence of long claws and relatively less bulbous toe tips.

Other sign: Disturbs ground litter by rooting as it looks for insects and grubs.

front
2.4 x 1.8 in
6 x 4.5 cm

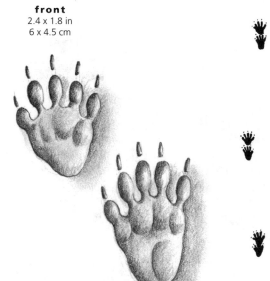

hind
2.8 x 1.8 in
7 x 4.5 cm

walk

FRONT TRACK LENGTH

FRONT TRACK WIDTH

Weasels
Mustela species

Long-tailed weasel
M. frenata

Two species
(ermine, *M.
erminea* and
long-tailed, *M.
frenata*), with long,
slender bodies, varying in size from a regular to a foot-long
hotdog. Pointed, flat skull with small ears. Males up to twice
as large as females. Largest males weigh about 1 lb (0.5 kg).
Overall color is brown, with a white belly. In winter, northern
individuals turn entirely white. Hairy, slender tail.

Track: Wide track. Five toes, in 1-3-1 grouping. Little toe, on inside of foot, often does not register. Interdigital pad chevron shaped. Heel seldom shows. Difficult to dis-
tinguish between species.

Trail: Galloping stride varies from 8–
30 in (20–75 cm). Side-by-side tracks,
when examined closely, show one
track slightly in front of the other—
a gallop. In snow, a drag mark may be found between front
and hind prints, sometimes forming a dumbbell shape.

Scat: Long, slender cord, usually with black, toothpaste-like animal
protein or hair. Cord tends to fold back on itself. Tapered at
both ends.

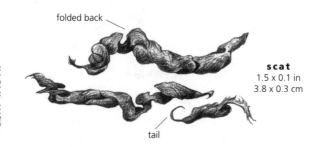

folded back

scat
1.5 x 0.1 in
3.8 x 0.3 cm

tail

SCAT WIDTH

Habitat: Prefer dense, low ground cover to open areas. Found in habitats where their prey, rodents, occur in high densities. Trails often lead from one rodent den to another. Travel in snow and ground burrows of other mammals.

Similar species: Differ from other mustelids by their smaller size and the drag mark commonly located between twin track patterns in the snow.

Other sign: Routes seldom follow a straight line, often having many sharp turns. Scat often deposited on raised objects.

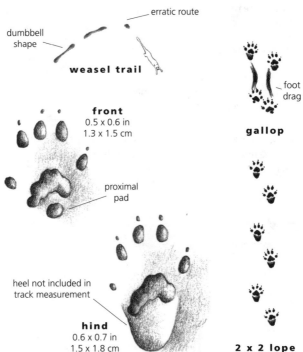

erratic route

dumbbell shape

weasel trail

front
0.5 x 0.6 in
1.3 x 1.5 cm

proximal pad

heel not included in track measurement

hind
0.6 x 0.7 in
1.5 x 1.8 cm

foot drag

gallop

2 x 2 lope

FRONT TRACK LENGTH

FRONT TRACK WIDTH

Spotted Skunk
Spilogale putorius

Black and white, the size of small domestic cat. Male weighs 1–2 lb (0.5–0.9 kg), female 0.5–1.25 lb (0.25–0.6 kg). Distinctive pattern of white spot on forehead, a spot by each ear, four white stripes along each side, and a white tip on tail. Spots and stripes highly variable.

Track: Size of a quarter, with longer claws on front footprint. Five toes, though 1-3-1 grouping is difficult to identify. Little toe, on the inside of foot, may not register. Clear front and hind prints on a hard surface may show a total of six hairless interdigital and proximal pads. Plantigrade heel on hind foot.

Trail: Loping stride is about 12 in (30 cm). Short bounds are very common. Often rambles as it walks, leaving a confused trail with most front and hind prints registering separately.

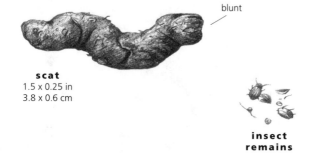

blunt

scat
1.5 x 0.25 in
3.8 x 0.6 cm

insect remains

Scat: Cylindrical, with blunt ends. Lacks the long taper and tendency to fold back on itself of other mustelid scat. May include mouse fur, bird feathers, insects, and carrion.

Habitat: Brush, chaparral, and open woodlands, especially along streams and in boulder areas.

Similar species: Distinguished from striped skunk by smaller track size and multiple foot pads.

Other sign: Nests in burrows beneath rock and wood piles or under buildings.

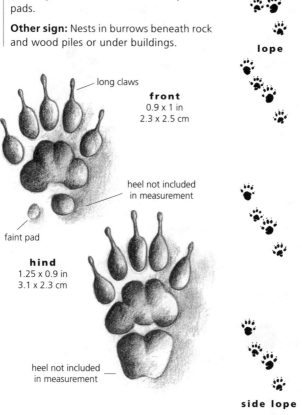

long claws

front
0.9 x 1 in
2.3 x 2.5 cm

heel not included in measurement

faint pad

hind
1.25 x 0.9 in
3.1 x 2.3 cm

heel not included in measurement

lope

side lope

FRONT TRACK LENGTH

FRONT TRACK WIDTH

Striped Skunk
Mephitis mephitis

Black-and-white mustelid, size of a domestic cat, with triangular head. Weight varies from 4–10 lb (2–5 kg). Male is slightly larger than female. Flat, wide, bushy tail with white hair on top. Long, curved claws for digging.

Track: Half dollar–sized, with long front claws. Hind track looks like a little human footprint. Five toes, in 1-3-1 grouping. Little toe, on the inside of foot, sometimes does not register. Interdigital pad chevron shaped. Proximal pad often shows. Hairless heel on hind foot.

Trail: Walking stride averages 12 in (30 cm). Meanders and stops often when walking, leaving "extra footprints" in trail. Lope may be turned to the side or straight forward.

Scat: Cylindrical with blunt ends. Lacks the long taper and tendency to fold back on itself of other mustelid scat. May be composed entirely of insect parts.

Habitat: Not habitat specific. Lives where burrows, cavities, or tunnels are present, including in and around buildings. Presence

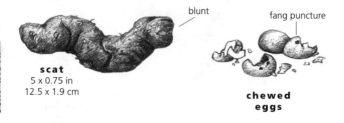

blunt

scat
5 x 0.75 in
12.5 x 1.9 cm

fang puncture

**chewed
eggs**

of insects and small mammals is critical to habitat selection.

Similar species: Differs from other species by having long, wide claws on the front foot. Front and hind tracks of skunk are smaller than those of badger. Front tracks of the skunk are similar in size to the back tracks, while the front tracks of the badger are much larger than its hind.

Other sign: Smell of skunk musk identifies nests and burrows. Tears apart nests of small mammals. Bird eggs show four fang punctures around larger hole in shell.

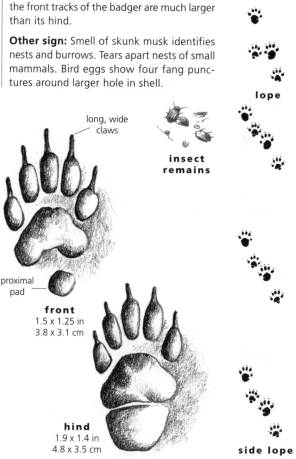

lope

long, wide claws

insect remains

proximal pad

front
1.5 x 1.25 in
3.8 x 3.1 cm

hind
1.9 x 1.4 in
4.8 x 3.5 cm

side lope

FRONT TRACK LENGTH

FRONT TRACK WIDTH

Badger
Taxidea taxus

Border collie–sized, with flat body, long hair, and long, shovel-like claws, about 18 lb (8 kg). Male 25 percent larger than female. Color varies from silver-gray to yellowish brown on back. Belly white. Feet are black or dark brown. White stripe down nose with black markings on sides of face. Short tail.

Track: Diameter of a golf ball, with long front claws, nearly as long as rest of footprint. Five toes, in 1-3-1 grouping. Little toe, on the inside of foot, sometimes does not register. Interdigital pad chevron shaped. Proximal pad often shows. Front footprint larger than hind.

Trail: Walking stride averages 14 in (35 cm). Walking is most common, but trotting, with a stride of 29 in (73 cm), occurs frequently.

Scat: Seldom found because deposited below ground in burrows. Similar to, but smaller than, coyote scat, without tapered ends.

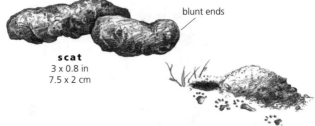

blunt ends

scat
3 x 0.8 in
7.5 x 2 cm

hole with dirt mound

SCAT WIDTH

Habitat: Open grasslands preferred. Areas with large populations of prey, which includes ground squirrels and prairie dogs.

Similar species: Differs from all other species by long claws on front foot and disproportionately small hind foot.

Other sign: Fresh excavations of large amounts of dirt from burrowing rodent holes indicates hunting activity, especially if excavated material includes large clods or rocks. Freshly widened burrow entrances may have a slightly elliptical shape. The presence of coyote and badger tracks together indicates cooperative hunting.

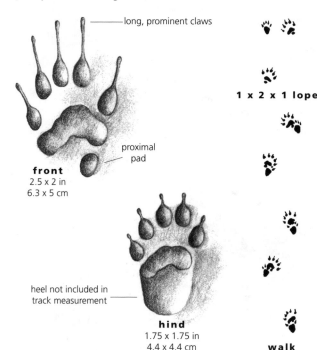

long, prominent claws

proximal pad

front
2.5 x 2 in
6.3 x 5 cm

1 x 2 x 1 lope

heel not included in track measurement

hind
1.75 x 1.75 in
4.4 x 4.4 cm

walk

Desert Cottontail
Sylvilagus auduboni

Medium-sized rabbit with large ears; weighs about 2 lb (0.9 kg). Body is gray and yellow, with a small white tuft of a tail. Other species of cottontails are found in this region, so look for the desert rabbit in the valleys.

Track: Toes asymmetrical around foot axis. Track indistinct because the foot is completely haired and lacks pads. Occasionally claws will register; these may be the only sign of a hopping rabbit. Hind footprint about two times longer than front.

Trail: Hoping stride is about 36 in (90 cm). Most of the time rabbits hop, but walking patterns will occasionally be observed.

Scat: Dry scat is a slightly flattened sphere. Produces a black, semiliquid scat usually re-ingested for remaining nutrients.

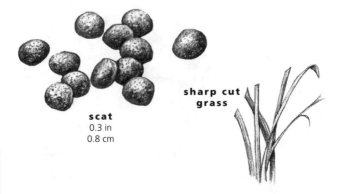

scat
0.3 in
0.8 cm

sharp cut grass

Habitat: Thick brush and chaparral interspersed with grass.

Similar species: Differs from jackrabbits and hare by having shorter heels and smaller overall size. Tracks of cottontail (*Sylvilagus*) species are often indistinguishable.

Other sign: Sharp incisors cleanly cut herbaceous vegetation at the height of a sitting rabbit, 4–6 in (10–20 cm). The cottontail's nest, known as a form, is a shallow depression in earth or grass.

walk

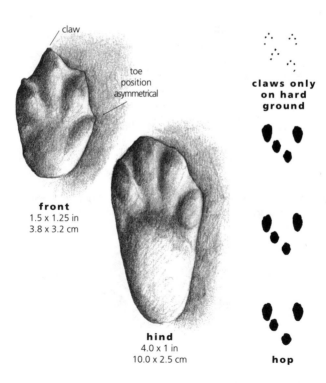

**claws only
on hard
ground**

front
1.5 x 1.25 in
3.8 x 3.2 cm

hind
4.0 x 1 in
10.0 x 2.5 cm

hop

claw

toe
position
asymmetrical

FRONT TRACK LENGTH

FRONT TRACK WIDTH

Black-tailed Jackrabbit
Lepus californicus

Large, slender hare with long (6 in / 15 cm) ears and large feet. Weighs 3–7 lb (1.4–3.2 kg). Body color is brownish gray. Tips of ears, top of tail, and rump are black. White-tailed jackrabbit *(L. townsendii)* of northern areas has a white tail, and may turn white in winter.

Track: Toes asymmetrical around foot axis. Track indistinct because the foot is completely haired and lacks pads. Claws occasionally register; on hard ground, they may be the only sign of a footprint. Hind footprint about three times longer than front. Footprints of white-tailed jackrabbit are about 10 percent longer.

Trail: Galloping stride may reach 10 feet (3 m). Tends to gallop rather than bound.

Scat: Dry scat is a slightly flattened sphere. Produces a black, semiliquid scat that is usually reingested to utilize remaining nutrients.

scat
0.3 in
0.8 cm

SCAT WIDTH

Habitat: Sparsely vegetated open areas of the desert and plains. White-tailed jackrabbit is found from plains grasslands to above tree line in the mountains.

Similar species: Differs from snowshoe hare by narrow width of hind print. Hind track differs from cottontail by greater length.

Other sign: Sharp incisors cleanly cut herbaceous vegetation at the height of a sitting rabbit, 4–6 in (10–15 cm). The jackrabbit's nest, known as a *form,* is a shallow depression, usually located under protective cover.

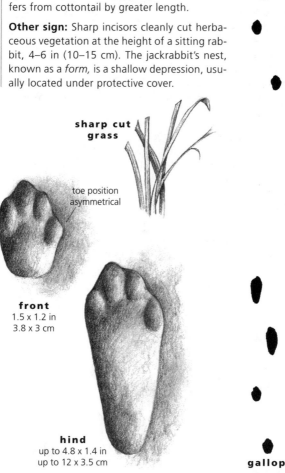

sharp cut grass

toe position asymmetrical

front
1.5 x 1.2 in
3.8 x 3 cm

hind
up to 4.8 x 1.4 in
up to 12 x 3.5 cm

gallop

FRONT TRACK LENGTH

FRONT TRACK WIDTH

Long-tailed vole
Microtus longicaudus

Mouse-sized mammal related to the lemming and weighing up to 1 oz (28 g). *Microtus* **are gray to gray-brown on back with a light colored belly. Stocky small mammals with short ears and small eyes almost hidden by their fur. Most voles have sparsely-haired, short tails but that of the long-tailed vole is over 2 in (5 cm).**

Track: Diminutive tracks smaller than a dime. Four toes on front foot, in 1-2-1 group. Five on hind foot, 1-3-1 grouping. Four joined interdigital and two proximal pads on front footprint and four interdigital pads and one proximal on hind footprint. Heel is hairless.

Trail: Trotting stride is 6 in (15 cm). Usually trots and seldom bounds. Tail usually does not show in the trail.

Scat: Typical mouse-shape ovals. Often placed in tennis ball–sized latrines consisting of thousands of pellets.

scat
0.1 in
0.2 cm

latrine

SCAT WIDTH

Habitat: Grass loving species found near meadows and water holes in dry country.

Similar species: Differ from shrews by having only four toes on the front feet. Differ from mice by seldom showing a tail drag and usually trotting.

Other sign: In the spring as snow melts, look for grass nests lacking entrances but having cords of grass and debris. Cords were made when grass and debris were stuffed inside tunnels in the snow. Latrines are usually found near nests. Voles make worn runways through the grass.

bound

fast trot

front
0.3 x 0.3 in
0.8 x 0.8 cm

hind
0.4 x 0.3 in
1 x 0.8 cm

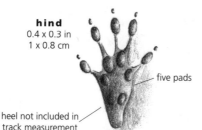

five pads

heel not included in track measurement

trot

Field Mouse

Peromyscus species

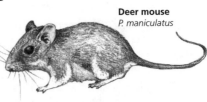

Deer mouse
P. maniculatus

Small mouse, weighing 0.5 oz (14 g). Adults are reddish brown on back with a white belly, while juveniles are dark gray on the back with a light gray belly. Large eyes and ears. Tail is long and haired.

Track: Track smaller than a dime. Four toes on front foot, in 1-2-1 grouping. Five toes on hind foot, 1-3-1 grouping. Four joined interdigital and two proximal pads on front footprint, five joined pads and heel on hind footprint. Heel is hairless.

Trail: Bounding stride averages 8 in (20 cm). Those species which use a full bound are climbers and nest in grass, shrubs, or trees. Those species using a half bound nest on or below ground. Both types occasionally trot. Tail drag may be present.

scat
0.1 in
0.3 cm

SCAT WIDTH

Scat: Oval-shaped pellets similar to those left by house mice.

Habitat: Found from deserts to the northern tree line, from below sea level to the top of high peaks. Wide range includes several species of field mice.

Similar species: Differs from shrew by having only four toes on the front feet and by being slightly larger. Differs from vole by often showing a tail drag and by most often bounding. Lacks the long heel of the jumping mouse. Smaller than chipmunk.

tail drag

Other sign: Compact grass nests without entrances may be found under logs, rocks, and boards. Enters and exits through the grass wall, which closes up after passage. Caches large quantities of seeds in any convenient protected area. Leaves feces near and in nest.

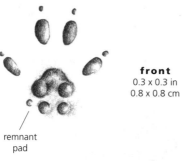

front
0.3 x 0.3 in
0.8 x 0.8 cm

remnant pad

4 x 4 bound

hind
0.4 x 0.3 in
1 x 0.8 cm

3 x 3 bound

FRONT TRACK LENGTH

FRONT TRACK WIDTH

Hispid Pocket Mouse
Perognathus hispidus

Large mouse, weighing 1–1.7 oz (28–48 g). Body color is mixed yellowish and brown. Hair is coarse. Tail shorter than head and body. Fur-lined, external check pouches. The hispid is largest of the pocket mice.

Track: Track about dime-sized though more data are needed. Four toes on front foot. Five toes on hind foot. The foot is hairy and prints are often indistinct.

Trail: Bound stride is about 8–10 in (20–25 cm). Uses a half bound.

Scat: Oval-shaped pellets similar to those left by house mice.

Habitat: Prefers sandy soils with short grass and other sparse vegetation.

scat
0.2 in
0.4 cm

Similar species: Differs from other mouse and vole species by indistinct track and occasional tail drag. Differs from shrews by having only four toes on front feet. Smaller than other rodent tracks.

Other sign: Burrows lack mounds. Stores caches of seeds often in depression on the ground surface.

front
about 0.4 x 0.4 in
1 x 1 cm

indistinct print

hind
0.5 x 0.4 in
1.3 x 1 cm

walk

FRONT TRACK LENGTH

FRONT TRACK WIDTH

Bannertail Kangaroo Rat

Dipodomys spectabilis

Size of a medium-sized house rat, weighing 4–10 oz (110–250 g). A spectacularly colored rat with a prominent long tail (8 in / 20 cm). Body brownish, peppered with black hairs. White stripe along side. Tail is black with narrow white side stripes and a white tip.

Track: Hind foot has four toes (some species have 5 toes). Long heel on hind foot may register. Feet are furred and toes may be difficult to distinguish.

Trail: Bounding stride about 20 in (50 cm). Often bounds on hind feet only. Tail drag often observed.

Scat: Small, usually unconnected ovals.

Habitat: Open, dry grasslands with brush and shrubs including mesquite and junipers.

scat
0.3 in
0.8 cm

SCAT WIDTH

Similar species: Differs from other kangaroo rats by the large size of the tracks. Differs from other mice by bounding on hind feet only—no front prints. Differs from most rodents by having only four toes in the hind track.

Other sign: Makes 10-foot diameter mounds from vegetation, debris, and dirt. Many openings lead to the den and seed caches. When people walk on the mounds, they often break through into the tunnels.

**bound on
hind feet**

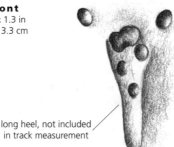

**tail drag
close-up**

front
1.3 x 1.3 in
3.3 x 3.3 cm

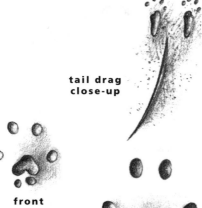

long heel, not included
in track measurement

hind
about 2 x 1 in
5 x 2.5 cm

bound

FRONT TRACK LENGTH

FRONT TRACK WIDTH

Ord's Kangaroo Rat
Dipodomys ordii

Stocky and mouse sized, about 2 oz (56 g), with large hind feet and long, fur-tipped tail. Reddish brown on back, white side stripe, and dark belly.

Track: Feet have four toes. Long heel on hind foot may register. Feet are furred and toes difficult to distinguish.

Trail: Bounding stride averages 7 in (18 cm) and typically ranges from 8–16 in (20–40 cm). Often bounds on hind feet only. Tail drag often observed.

Scat: Small, usually unconnected ovals.

Habitat: Low-elevation animal. Prefers sandy soil where it can easily dig burrows.

scat
0.2 in
0.5 cm

SCAT WIDTH

Similar species: Track differs from western jumping mouse by greater width and more hair. Bounds on the hind feet only; no front prints visible in the bounding pattern.

Other sign: Scrapes out shallow "bathtubs" in dust as it dusts itself for protection against fleas.

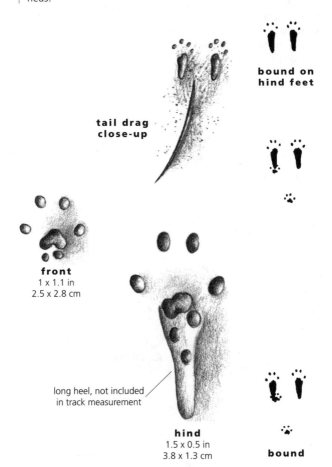

bound on hind feet

tail drag close-up

front
1 x 1.1 in
2.5 x 2.8 cm

long heel, not included in track measurement

hind
1.5 x 0.5 in
3.8 x 1.3 cm

bound

Colorado Chipmunk
Tamias quadrivittatus

Slightly larger than a large mouse, up to 3 oz (85 g). Reddish fur, with white stripes bordered by black stripes along the sides of the face and body. Haired tail.

Track: Nickel-sized front foot, with four toes in a 1-2-1 grouping. Five toes on hind foot, 1-3-1 grouping. Toes relatively slender. Claws short. Hind heel is haired and details in the track are difficult to detect.

Trail: Bounding stride averages 7 in (18 cm). Mostly terrestrial, it usually uses a half bound, though full bounds may be observed.

Scat: Small, usually unconnected ovals.

scat
0.1 in
0.3 cm

SCAT WIDTH

Habitat: Varies, including coniferous forest and shrubland. Usually found near rocks.

Similar species: Smaller than ground and tree squirrels. Lacks the long claws of the ground squirrels and prairie dog. Tracks of chipmunk (*Tamias*) species are indistinguishable.

Other sign: Seeds and nuts of various plants, chewed open on one side.

front
0.5 x 0.4 in
1.3 x 1 cm

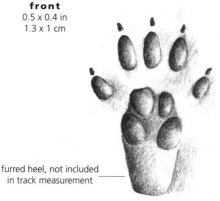

furred heel, not included in track measurement

hind
0.7 x 0.6 in
1.8 x 1.5 cm

half bound

FRONT TRACK LENGTH

FRONT TRACK WIDTH

Mexican Woodrat

Neotoma mexicana

Size of a small house rat, weighing about 0.3–0.5 lb (150–225 g). Body is gray, belly white, tail white below and blackish above. Relatively large ears. Hairless tail.

Track: Four toes with 1-2-1 spacing on front foot and five with a 1-3-1 on hind foot. Toes are relatively slender and toe pads slightly constricted. Three joined interdigital, one remnant, and two proximal pads in front footprint and four interdigital palm pads and two proximal pads in hind footprint. Feet have considerable hair, sometimes making prints appear indistinct and large.

Trail: Bounding stride is 10 in (25 cm) and walking stride is 6 in (15 cm). Bounding is probably the most common gait but woodrats also commonly walk.

Scat: Small oval pellets.

nest

scat
0.2 in
0.4 cm

Habitat: Prefers woodlands with rocky sites or cliffs. Also more in montane areas with mixed coniferous forests. Presence of rocks may be key.

Similar species: Larger than mice and voles. Differs from squirrels by the presence of heel pads on hind foot. Tracks of woodrat (*Neotoma*) species are indistinguishable.

Other sign: Constructs nests of sticks, cactus, bone, porcupine quills, and other debris in cracks in the rocks and below ground. Large amounts of deposited and dried feces, called a midden, signal their presence. Middens may be 100,000 years old.

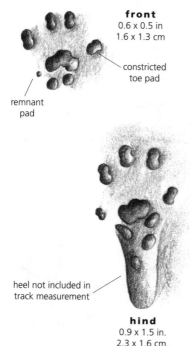

front
0.6 x 0.5 in
1.6 x 1.3 cm

constricted toe pad

remnant pad

heel not included in track measurement

hind
0.9 x 1.5 in.
2.3 x 1.6 cm.

bound

fast walk

FRONT TRACK LENGTH

FRONT TRACK WIDTH

White-throated Woodrat
Neotoma albigula

Size of a large house rat, weighing about 5–10 oz (140–280 g). Hairless long tail is white below and brown above. Back gray to reddish, belly and throat white to light gray.

Track: Four toes with 1-2-1 spacing on front foot and five with a 1-3-1 on hind foot. Toes relatively slender, and toe pads slightly constricted. Three joined interdigital, one remnant, and two proximal pads in front footprint and four interdigital palm pads and two proximal pads on hind print. Feet hairy, sometimes making prints appear indistinct and large.

Trail: Bounding stride is 14 in (36 cm) and walking stride is 6 in (15 cm). Bounding is probably the most common gait but woodrats also commonly walk.

Scat: Small oval pellets.

scat
0.2 in
0.4 cm

nest

Habitat: Arid grasslands and shrub country usually with cactus.

Similar species: Larger than mice and voles. Differs from squirrels by the presence of heel pads on hind foot.

Other sign: Constructs aboveground nests around the base of cactus using cactus spines and joints.

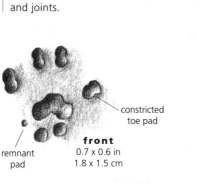

constricted toe pad

front
0.7 x 0.6 in
1.8 x 1.5 cm

remnant pad

bound

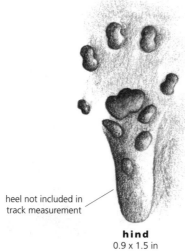

heel not included in track measurement

hind
0.9 x 1.5 in
2.3 x 1.6 cm

fast walk

FRONT TRACK LENGTH

FRONT TRACK WIDTH

Rock Squirrel
Spermophilus variegatus

Size of a large rat,
weighing about
1.5 lb (700 g).
Body is mottled
gray mixed with
red and brown. Head
and back may be very dark.
Long, bushy tail.

Track: Four toes with 1-2-1 grouping on front footprint and five toes
with 1-3-1 spacing on hind. Toes relatively slender. Front footprint size of
a quarter. Hind heel is hairless and
may register clearly in track. Claws
may show. More data are needed on
track size.

Trail: Bounding stride averages 25 in (65 cm). Uses a half bound,
showing its terrestrial lifestyle.

scat
0.2 in
0.5 cm

burrow entrance

Scat: Small ovals, usually not connected.

Habitat: Rocky areas with low vegetation in grasslands and open woodlands. Not found under dense timber or chaparral. Uses large boulders for lookout posts.

Similar species: *Spermophilus* species can not be differentiated from each other by tracks. Habitat and visual identification necessary. Claws longer and feet smaller than those of tree squirrels. Lack the long claws of prairie dogs. Smaller than marmot.

Other sign: Dens under large boulders. A loud, sharp whistle warns of danger and gives away its presence.

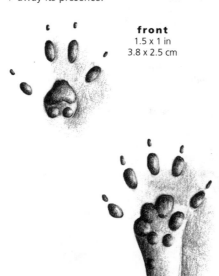

front
1.5 x 1 in
3.8 x 2.5 cm

hairless heel, not included in track measurement

hind
2.0 x 1.6 in
5.0 x 4.0 cm

bound

Abert's Squirrel "Tassle-eared Squirrel"

Sciurus aberti

Large squirrel,
weighing up to 2
lb (4.4 kg). Body
and tail color
variable. Back
reddish, sides
gray, belly white or
black. Tail may be all
white or only white beneath. Large reddish ear tufts except
during late summer. Tail haired.

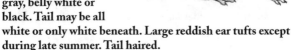

Track: Front foot size of a quarter, with four toes in a 1-2-1 grouping. Five toes on hind foot, 1-3-1 grouping. Toes relatively slender. Claws short. More data are needed on track size.

Trail: Bounding stride about 30 in (75 cm).

scat
0.2 in
0.5 cm

**chewed cones
and seed
casings**

Scat: Small, shapeless black masses to small, usually unconnected ovals.

Habitat: Restricted to ponderosa pine forests.

Similar species: Larger than chipmunk. Lacks the long, digging claws of ground squirrels. Differentiation from tree squirrels is only possible based on habitat

Other sign: Uses large nests located high in pine trees. Its call may give its presence away.

hind prints on front

slow bound

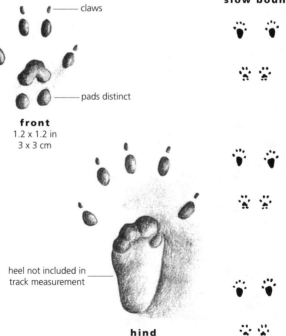

claws

front
1.2 x 1.2 in
3 x 3 cm

pads distinct

heel not included in track measurement

hind
2.75 x 1.3 in
6.9 x 3.3 cm

full bound

FRONT TRACK LENGTH

FRONT TRACK WIDTH

Plains Pocket Gopher
Geomys bursarius

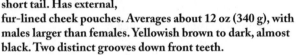

Guinea pig–
sized rodent
with minute eyes
and ears and a
short tail. Has external,
fur-lined cheek pouches. Averages about 12 oz (340 g), with
males larger than females. Yellowish brown to dark, almost
black. Two distinct grooves down front teeth.

Track: Five toes front and hind foot. Toes are relatively slender. Front feet have relatively long, wide claws for digging. Claw length is equal to or longer than toe length. Good tracks are seldom found and more data are needed on track size. Measurements are approximate.

Trail: Walking stride is 6 in (15 cm).

Scat: Thick, short cords.

Habitat: Needs deep sandy soils preferably associated with grasslands, meadows, and fields.

Similar species: Differs from other rodents by large, wide claws.

SCAT WIDTH

scat
0.2 in
0.5 cm

Other sign: Summer mounds consist of loose dirt forming a flat mound with no entrance visible (gophers close the tunnel as they go back underground). Winter casts of soil and rocks show where gophers packed dirt into snow tunnels while they burrowed for food. Scats are often found in the tunnel casts.

prominent claws

fast walk

front
0.8 x 0.7 in
2 x 1.8 cm

heel not included in track measurement

hind
1 x 0.7 in
2.5 x 1.8 cm

walk

FRONT TRACK LENGTH

FRONT TRACK WIDTH

Prairie Dog
Cynomys species

Black-tailed prairie dog
C. ludovicianus

Size of a large guinea pig, 2–3 lb (1–1.4 kg). Fat, yellowish brown ground squirrel. The black-tailed prairie dog (*C. ludovicianus*) has a black-tipped tail, the white-tail (*C. leucurus*) a white-tipped tail. The white-tail lives northwest of the range shown for black-tail. Lives in large colonies.

Track: Size of a quarter dollar. Long claws on front prints for digging. Four toes on front track, in 1-2-1 grouping (toe 5 does not show). Five toes on hind track, 1-3-1 grouping. Toes are relatively slender.

Trail: Bounding stride averages 30 in (75 cm). Uses a half bound. Trots more than other squirrels.

Scat: Ranges from oval to a cord five to six times longer than wide. Scats often connected by narrow filaments.

linked

scat
0.1–0.2 in
0.3–0.5 cm

mound and hole

SCAT WIDTH

Habitat: Prairie and open grassland, where colony may consist of thousands of acres of low dirt mounds concealing tunnels.

Similar species: Differs from ground squirrel by the presence of longer digging claws. Claws longer and broader and feet smaller than those of tree squirrels. Smaller than marmot. Larger than mouse and vole.

Other sign: Colonies consisting of many burrows with elevated mounds and manicured "lawns" of grazed grass.

side lope

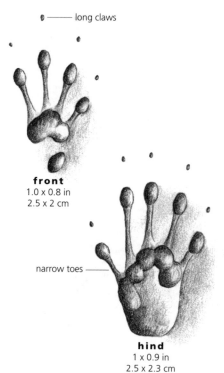

⊙ —— long claws

front
1.0 x 0.8 in
2.5 x 2 cm

narrow toes ——

hind
1 x 0.9 in
2.5 x 2.3 cm

bound

FRONT TRACK LENGTH

FRONT TRACK WIDTH

Muskrat
Ondatra zibethica

Large, rat-like, stocky, up to 4 lb (2 kg). Males slightly larger than females. Small eyes and ears. Tail is black, flattened, scaly, with few hairs.

Track: Four toes on front foot (small fifth nubbin may show in very clear tracks) and five on hind foot. Toes very slender. Hind foot appears wider than long.

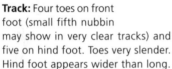

Trail: Walking strides averages 11 in (28 cm). May lope with body turned to side.

Scat: Oval, at most three to four times longer than wide. Often deposited in a sticky mass on exposed logs at water's edge.

Habitat: Marshes and lake edges, secondarily on stream banks. Large rivers are not as frequently used.

scat
0.2 in
0.5 cm

SCAT WIDTH

Similar species: Differs from beaver by smaller size and lack of webbing. Differs from mink by long slender toes and by usually walking.

Other sign: Small conical domes made from reeds serve as dens. Cut grass and reeds near water's edge mark feeding sites. Muskrats make "post offices," repeated scat deposits, on rocks.

4 x 4 bound

3 x 3 bound

post office

front
1.3 x 1.2 in
3.3 x 3 cm

side lope

— wide foot —

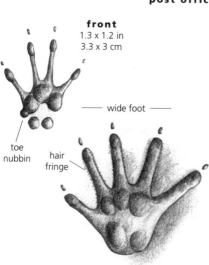

toe nubbin   hair fringe

fast walk

hind
1.3 x 1.6 in
3.3 x 4 cm

walk

FRONT TRACK LENGTH

FRONT TRACK WIDTH

Yellow-bellied Marmot
Marmota flaviventris

Size of a large, fat domestic cat, 5–15 lb (2–7 kg). Male larger than female. Ears and head are short and broad. Tail about one-third body length. Color brown to yellowish brown on back, but yellow on belly.

Track: Front foot size of a silver dollar, with four toes in 1-2-1 grouping. Five toes on hind foot, 1-3-1 grouping. Toes relatively slender. Four joined interdigital and two proximal pads on front footprint, and four joined interdigital pads on hind foot. Heel is hairless.

Trail: Bounding stride varies from 24 in (60 cm) to 50 in (125 cm). A ground dweller, the marmot uses a half bound.

Scat: Wide variety of forms, from oval pellets to long cords, all of which may be tightly stuck together. Sometimes lacks defined shape, being dark and runny when deposited. Deposited in "latrines" or "post offices" on top of prominent rocks and along ledges.

scat
0.25–0.5 in
0.6–1.3 cm

scat on rocks

Habitat: High mountain areas, especially those with talus and boulder fields. Larger boulders that protect tunnels against digging predators are preferred.

Similar species: Largest of the squirrels, its track dwarfs other ground squirrels. Track left when drinking at a stream may be distinguished from beaver's by lack of webbing and by having only four toes on front prints.

Other sign: May dig tunnels in non-rocky ground between boulder fields, probably as escape tunnels to be used when moving between rocky areas.

proximal pads

front
2.2 x 1.8 in
5.5 x 4.5 cm

hind
2.8 x 2 in
7 x 5 cm

bound

Porcupine
Erethizon dorsatum

Basketball-sized or larger, 10–25 lb (5–11 kg). Stocky body, with short legs. Distinguished by the presence of quills. Brown to yellowish brown in color.

Track: Rough texture formed by small nubs on soles of feet. Four toes on front foot and five toes on hind. Toes often do not show.

Trail: Walking stride 17 in (43 cm). Tail drag often present.

Scat: Winter scat formed from feeding on conifers is red. Summer scat

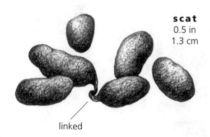

scat
0.5 in
1.3 cm

linked

debarked stick with chew marks

includes more herbs and shrubs, and is brown to black. Scat from both seasons may be composed of individual pellets or strings of pellets connected by fibers.

Habitat: Generally found near forests, but may be far from trees if shrubs are available.

Similar species: Rough texture on sole of foot is diagnostic. In snow, trough made by dragging belly highlights its stockiness, separating it from faster-moving mammals.

Other sign: Twigs with bark chewed off, found around tree bases. Will perch in a tree for days, chewing the bark, and killing the tree.

tail drag

fast walk

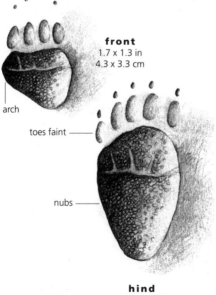

front
1.7 x 1.3 in
4.3 x 3.3 cm

arch

toes faint

nubs

hind
2.7 x 1.7 in
6.8 x 4.3 cm

walk

FRONT TRACK LENGTH

FRONT TRACK WIDTH

Beaver
Castor canadensis

Largest rodent in North America, 30–60 lb (14–27 kg). Distinguished by large, webbed hind feet and large, horizontally flattened tail. Fur overall is dark brown to almost black, with lighter belly.

Track: Front and hind prints show five toes. Hind foot may be larger than a human hand. Webbing between hind toes shows, but only when pulled tight by splaying of toes. Clear tracks are difficult to find, as the hind foot steps on the front foot and the dragging tail obliterates many prints.

Trail: Walking stride 18 in (45 cm).

Scat: Seldom found, as they are usually deposited in water, where they disintegrate quickly. Marshmallow-sized, a little longer than thick. Consist of wood chips.

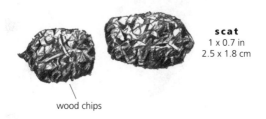

scat
1 x 0.7 in
2.5 x 1.8 cm

wood chips

SCAT WIDTH

Habitat: Seldom found far from a creek, river, pond, or lake.

Similar species: Differs from other rodents by large size and webbing. Differs from river otter by long, slender toes and pointed heel, and by lacking a chevron-shaped pad.

Other sign: Dams and conical lodges, built of twigs and sticks. Standing, cut-off tree trunks end in a tapered cone. Debarked tree limbs in the water.

lodge

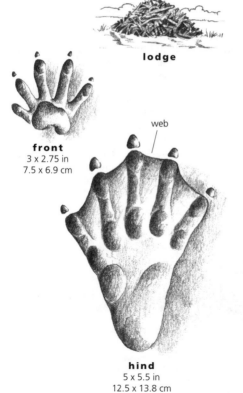

web

front
3 x 2.75 in
7.5 x 6.9 cm

hind
5 x 5.5 in
12.5 x 13.8 cm

walk

FRONT TRACK LENGTH

FRONT TRACK WIDTH

Collared Peccary "Javelina"
Dicotyles tajacu

Collie-sized, weighing up to 50 lb (23 kg). North America's wild pig–like mammal has mixed black and gray, coarse hair on the body. A white, often faint, collar rings the neck over the shoulders.

Track: Silver dollar–sized tracks with each clout rounded and blunt at the tip. Flat-bottomed hooves often do not leave much of a mark on the ground. Two dew claws on front foot but only one on hind foot.

Trail: Walking stride is 23 in (60 cm). The walking trail is often a set of rambling prints with many tracks registering close together as the javelina turns from side to side. Trotting stride is about 30 in (80 cm). Its strange "rocking horse" gallop is a slow lope, but gallops may reach 100 in (250 cm).

scat
1.2 x 1.6 in
3 x 1.4 cm

Scat: Consist of dry vegetation chips. Scat shape varies from oval to about 3 times longer than wide.

Habitat: Usually found near water holes or in dry streambeds. Prefers chaparral including oaks, mesquites, and cactus.

Similar species: Differs from deer by their blunt, rounded tips and rambling trails.

Other sign: The desert floor often shows disturbances caused while rooting for roots, nuts, fruits, insects, and eggs.

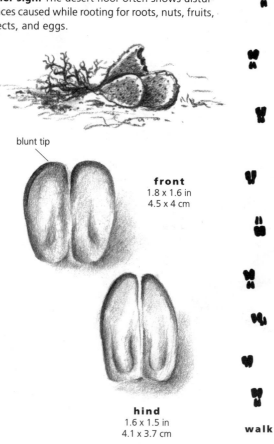

blunt tip

front
1.8 x 1.6 in
4.5 x 4 cm

hind
1.6 x 1.5 in
4.1 x 3.7 cm

walk

FRONT TRACK LENGTH

FRONT TRACK WIDTH

White-tailed Deer
Odocoileus virginianus

Smallest member of the deer family. Male averages 130 lb (60 kg), female about 110 lb (50 kg). Coat is reddish in summer and blue-gray in winter. The prominent white tail is carried erect when animal disturbed. Antlers, found only on male, have *tines*, or points, branching off main beam.

Track: Heart shaped, with convex wall. Pad occupies most of the clout; subunguinis slender.

Trail: Walking stride 30 in (75 cm). Pronks or stots with front and hind feet striking the ground at the same time. Gallops when in a hurry.

Scat: Usually dry, falls apart when it hits the ground. Pellets vary from nipple-dimple shape to oval.

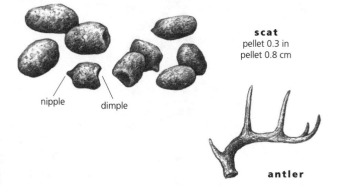

nipple

dimple

scat
pellet 0.3 in
pellet 0.8 cm

antler

SCAT WIDTH

Habitat: Generally closed timber, but moves out to grasslands at twilight to feed.

Similar species: Track is not distinguishable from mule deer, although whitetail is usually smaller in most geographic areas. Differs from pronghorn, goats, and sheep by having convex walls. Smaller than elk, has more slender tips, and pad occupies most of clout.

Other sign: Gathers ("yards up") in large numbers in sheltered groves during the winter. Breaks off limbs of trees when removing the velvet from antlers. Velvet is difficult to find, as both deer and rodents eat the nutrient-rich material. Height of tree wound indicates animal height.

pronk

subunguinis very narrow

convex wall

front
3 x 1.9 in
7.5 x 4.8 cm

hind
2.6 x 1.5 in
6.5 x 3.8 cm

gallop

FRONT TRACK LENGTH

FRONT TRACK WIDTH

Mule Deer
Odocoileus hemionus

Small member of the
deer family, male
averaging 160 lb
(70 kg) and female
about 130 lb (60 kg).
Coat color is reddish
brown in summer and
grayish brown in the
winter. Antlers, found
only on males, branch
symmetrically and are
shed annually.

Track: Heart shaped, with convex
wall. Pad occupies most of the clout;
subunguinis slender.

Trail: Walking stride 36 in (90 cm).
Pronks or stots with front and hind
feet striking the ground at the same
time. Gallops when in a hurry.

Scat: Usually dry, falls apart when it
hits the ground. Pellets vary from nipple-dimple shape to oval.

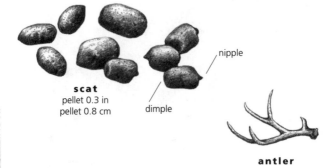

scat
pellet 0.3 in
pellet 0.8 cm

nipple

dimple

antler

Habitat: Foothills are prime habitat, where can frequent open brush interspersed with rugged terrain. Found in all vegetation zones except in the Arctic and in extreme desert.

Similar species: Track is not distinguishable from white-tailed deer, although mule deer is usually larger in most geographic areas. Differs from pronghorn, goats, and sheep by having convex walls. Smaller than elk, has more slender tips, and pad occupies most of clout.

Other sign: Breaks off limbs of trees when removing the velvet from antlers. Velvet is difficult to find, as both deer and rodents eat the nutrient-rich material. Height of tree wound indicates height of animal.

pronk

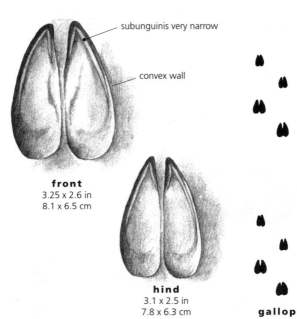

subunguinis very narrow

convex wall

front
3.25 x 2.6 in
8.1 x 6.5 cm

hind
3.1 x 2.5 in
7.8 x 6.3 cm

gallop

FRONT TRACK LENGTH

FRONT TRACK WIDTH

Pronghorn "American Antelope"

Antilocapra americana

Smaller than deer, found only in North America. Male averages 125 lb (56 kg), female about 110 lb (50 kg). White and tan to reddish brown, with black and brown markings on the head and neck. Both sexes have forked horns that are shed annually.

Track: Identified by the concave outline of the wall, which bends slightly inward at a point about one-third of the way back from the tip. Pad is bulbous. Lacks dewclaws.

Trail: Ambling stride 35 in (88 cm). Most common gait is an amble, a fast walk where the hind foot registers slightly in front of the front footprint. Often uses a Z-shaped gallop, with a stride ranging from 80–145 in (200–363 cm).

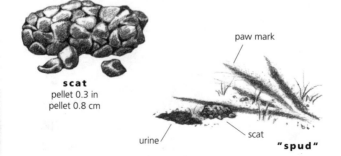

scat
pellet 0.3 in
pellet 0.8 cm

paw mark

urine

scat

"spud"

SCAT WIDTH

Scat: Well-defined pellets that often stay together upon impact with the ground.

Habitat: Open and shrub country of short- to mid-grass prairie. Herbs and winter browse above the snow are important. Commonly found with sagebrush. In their wide range, populations are scattered only in favorable habitat.

Similar species: Differentiated from deer by its small size and concave wall. Lacks dew-claws.

Other sign: The territorial marking of the male pronghorn is a *spud*, produced as the male **s**niffs and **p**aws the ground after **u**rinating and **d**efecating to spread the odor.

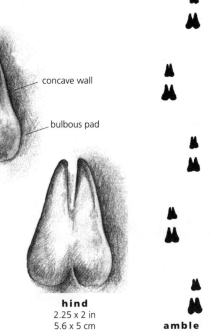

gallop

concave wall

bulbous pad

front
2.75 x 2.25 in
6.9 x 5.6 cm

hind
2.25 x 2 in
5.6 x 5 cm

amble

FRONT TRACK LENGTH

FRONT TRACK WIDTH

Elk

Cervus elaphus

Medium-sized, larger than deer, males averaging 700 lb (315 kg) and females 450 lb (200 kg). Reddish to dark brown, with a yellow rump patch. Males shed antlers annually. Also known as wapiti.

Track: Blocky, with each clout wide at the leading tip. Pad of hoof occupies rear third of each clout; subunguinis occupies remaining two-thirds of each clout.

Trail: Walking stride 52 in (130 cm). When chased by a predator, gallops and occasionally pronks.

Scat: Most of the year, scat consists of pellets that scatter on impact with the ground. When the diet is moist, nipple-dimple

nipple

dimple

scat
pellet 0.5 in
pellet 1.3 cm

antler

shape predominates, changing to oval as vegetation dries. When scat is moist, pellets stick together.

Habitat: Forest. Beds in dense trees during the day, moving out into clearings to graze during twilight hours.

pronk

Similar species: Differs from deer and moose by having a small pad at the rear of the hoof. Differs from bighorn sheep and antelope by having walls that bend to the outside of each clout.

Other sign: Removing antler velvet, bulls strip bark from young saplings and break off limbs, often killing the trees. Height of tree wound shows animal height. Bulls make mud wallows in the fall. During rut, look for areas where bulls have sparred with the ground using their antlers.

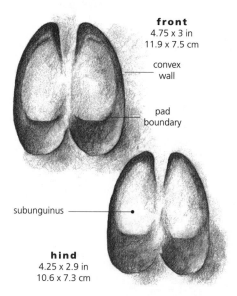

front
4.75 x 3 in
11.9 x 7.5 cm

convex wall

pad boundary

subunguinus

hind
4.25 x 2.9 in
10.6 x 7.3 cm

gallop

FRONT TRACK LENGTH

Desert Bighorn Sheep

Ovis c. californiana

Medium-sized sheep distinguished by males with massive horns. Horns of rams are spiraled and those of ewes small and straight. Sheep horns are not forked and are never shed. Males weigh about 180–200 lb (80–90 kg), about 100 lb (45 kg) less than their northern relatives. Color is light brown with a white rump and muzzle.

Track: Blocky with edges of the walls straight along the sides.

Trail: Trotting stride is 70 in (180 cm). Most common gait is a walk, but trotting is common in open country.

Scat: Tend to be dry and separate into individual pellets more than those of other hooved mammals.

Habitat: Found in high mountain areas, especially along cliffs. Graze on grass in rolling hills and come down from cliffs to reach a source of water. In their wide range, populations are scattered only in favorable habitat.

Similar species: Differ from antelope and deer by having a straight edge to the wall. Bighorn sheep tracks may show dew

SCAT WIDTH

scat
pellet 0.3 in
pellet 0.8 cm

claws while those of the pronghorn never show dew claws because pronghorn do not have dew claws on their legs. Subunguinis region of the hoof is relatively large.

Other sign: Repeatedly use bed along the edges of cliffs and deposits of old scats may be considerable. Mineral or salt licks often serve as a focus of sheep activity.

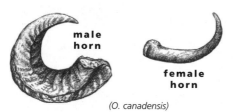

male horn

female horn

(O. canadensis)

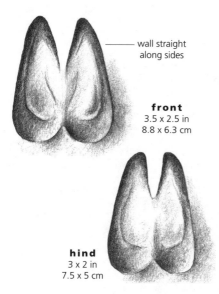

wall straight along sides

front
3.5 x 2.5 in
8.8 x 6.3 cm

hind
3 x 2 in
7.5 x 5 cm

trot

FRONT TRACK LENGTH

FRONT TRACK WIDTH

Selected reading

Tracks and Tracking

Bang, P. et al. 1972. *Collins Guide to Animal Tracks and Signs.* London: Collins Sons.

Brown, R., J. Ferguson, M. Lawrence, and D. Lees. 1987. *Tracks and Signs of the Birds of Britain and Europe: An Identification Guide.* Kent, England: Christopher Helm.

Brunner, J. 1909. *Tracks and Tracking.* New York: Outing.

Fjelline, D. P. and T. M. Mansfield. 1989. Method to standardize the procedure for measuring mountain lion tracks. In *Proceedings of the Third Mountain Lion Workshop,* ed. R.H. Smith, 49–51. Prescott, Ariz.: Arizona Game and Fish Department.

Forrest, L. R. 1988. *Field Guide to Tracking Animals in Snow.* Harrisburg, Penn.: Stackpole Books.

Halfpenny, J. C. 1997. *Tracking: Mastering the Basics.* 180 min. A Naturalist's World. Videocassette.

———— 1986a. *A Field Guide to Mammal Tracking in North America.* Boulder, Colo.: Johnson.

———— 1986b. *Tracks and Tracking: A "How To" Guide.* Gardiner, Mont.: A Naturalist's World. Slides.

Halfpenny, J. C. et al. 1996. Snow tracking. In *American Marten, Fisher, Lynx, and Wolverines: Survey Methods for Their Detection,* ed. W. Zielinski and T. Kucera, 91–163. General Technical Report PSW-GTR-157. Berkeley, Calif.: USDA Forest Service, Pacific Southwest Research Station.

Headstrom, R. 1971. *Identifying Animals Tracks: Mammals, Birds, and Other Animals of the Eastern United States.* New York: Dover.

Murie, O. 1954. *A Field Guide to Animal Tracks.* Peterson Field Guide Series, no. 9. Boston: Houghton Mifflin.

Rezendes, P. 1999. *Tracking and the Art of Seeing: How to Read Animal Tracks and Sign.* 2nd Ed.. Charlotte, Vt.: Camden House.

Seton, E. T. 1958. *Animal Tracks and Hunter Signs.* New York: Doubleday.

Recommended field identification guides

Burt, W. H. and R. P. Grossenheider. 1964. *A Field Guide to the Mammals.* Peterson Field Guide Series, no. 5. Boston: Houghton Mifflin.

Chandlers, S. R., B. Bruun, H. S. Zim. 1983. *A Guide to Field Identification: Birds of North America.* New York: Golden.

National Geographic Society. 1983. *Field Guide to the Birds of North America.* Washington, D.C.: National Geographic Society.

Stebbins, R. C. 1966. *A Field Guide to Western Reptiles and Amphibians.* Peterson Field Guide Series, no. 16. Boston: Houghton Mifflin.

Index

About the author

JAMES HALFPENNY has searched for dinosaur tracks in Colorado and Montana, tracked wildlife in Tanzania and Kenya, studied endangered species on China's Tibet-Qinghai plateau, and researched the polar bears of Hudson Bay and Greenland. Since 1961 he has taught outdoor and environmental education for a vast array of schools and organizations, including the Smithsonian, National Outdoor Leadership School, Outward Bound, the Appalachian Mountain Club, The Wilderness Society, National Wildlife Federation, Defenders of Wildlife, and National Audubon Society. He has trained rangers in tracking techniques at Yellowstone, Glacier, Grand Teton, and Rocky Mountain national parks. His research has also taken him to Antarctica and all over North America. Halfpenny has been featured, with Australian aborigines, Kalahari Bushmen, and Alaskan Inuits, in a documentary about the loss of native tracking skills shown on the Discovery Channel. He is a past field director and project coordinator for the University of Colorado's Institute of Arctic and Alpine Research. He is also the author of *Scats and Tracks of the Pacific Coast, Scats and Tracks of the Rocky Mountains, A Field Guide to Mammal Tracking in North America, Discovering Yellowstone Wolves: Watcher's Guide,* and *Winter: an Ecological Handbook.* He lives just outside Yellowstone National Park in Gardiner, Montana.

About the illustrator

TODD TELANDER is a freelance natural science illustrator and wildlife artist. He studied biology and environmental studies at the University of California, Santa Cruz, where he became interested in illustration. His work appears in Falcon's *America's 100 Most Wanted Birds, Birder's Dictionary, A Field Guide to Cows,* and *A Field Guide to Pigs* as well as in museums, galleries, and private collections. Telander lives in Trinidad, California.

Notes

Notes

Notes

Notes

Notes

Notes

Notes

Notes

get
FALCON GUIDED

Field Guides

Bitterroot: Montana State Flower
Canyon Country Wildflowers
Central Rocky Mountain Wildflowers
Chihuahuan Desert Wildflowers
Great Lakes Berry Book
New England Berry Book
Ozark Wildflowers
Pacific Northwest Berry Book
Plants of Arizona
Rare Plants of Colorado
Rocky Mountain Berry Book
Scats & Tracks of the Pacific Coast
Scats & Tracks of the Rocky Mountains
Sierra Nevada Wildflowers
Southern Rocky Mountain Wildflowers
Tallgrass Prairie Wildflowers
Western Trees

FALCON GUIDES ®Leading the Way™

All books in this popular series are regularly updated with accurate information on access, side trips, & safety.

HIKING GUIDES

Best Hikes Along the Continental Divide
Exploring Canyonlands & Arches
Exploring Hawaii's Parklands
Exploring Mount Helena
Exploring Southern California Beaches
Hiking Alaska
Hiking Arizona
Hiking Arizona's Cactus Country
Hiking the Beartooths
Hiking Big Bend National Park
Hiking the Bob Marshall Country
Hiking California
Hiking California's Desert Parks
Hiking Carlsbad Caverns & Guadalupe
   Mtns. National Parks
Hiking Colorado
Hiking Colorado, Vol. II
Hiking Colorado's Summits
Hiking Colorado's Weminuche Wilderness
Hiking the Columbia River Gorge
Hiking Florida
Hiking Georgia
Hiking Glacier/Waterton Lakes
Hiking Grand Canyon National Park
Hiking Grand Staircase-Escalante
Hiking Grand Teton National Park
Hiking Great Basin
Hiking Hot Springs of the Pacific NW
Hiking Idaho
Hiking Indiana
Hiking Maine
Hiking Maryland and Delaware
Hiking Michigan
Hiking Minnesota
Hiking Montana
Hiking Mount Rainier National Park
Hiking Mount St. Helens
Hiking Nevada
Hiking New Hampshire

Hiking New Mexico
Hiking New York
Hiking North Carolina
Hiking North Cascades
Hiking Northern Arizona
Hiking Northern California
Hiking Olympic National Park
Hiking Oregon
Hiking Oregon's Central Cascades
Hiking Oregon's Eagle Cap Wilderness
Hiking Oregon's Mt Hood/Badger Creek
Hiking Pennsylvania
Hiking Ruins Seldom Seen
Hiking Shenandoah National Park
Hiking the Sierra Nevada
Hiking South Carolina
Hiking South Dakota's Black Hills Cntry
Hiking Southern New England
Hiking Tennessee
Hiking Texas
Hiking Utah
Hiking Utah's Summits
Hiking Vermont
Hiking Virginia
Hiking Washington
Hiking Wyoming
Hiking Wyoming's Cloud Peak
   Wilderness
Hiking Wyoming's Teton and Washakie
   Wilderness
Hiking Wyoming's Wind River Range
Hiking Yellowstone National Park
Hiking Yosemite
Hiking Zion & Bryce Canyon
Wild Country Companion
Wild Montana
Wild Utah
Wild Virginia
Wilderness Directory

FALCON®

FALCON GUIDES ® Leading the Way™

FALCON GUIDES ® are available for where-to-go hiking, mountain biking, rock climbing, walking, scenic driving, fishing, rockhounding, paddling, birding, wildlife viewing, and camping. We also have FalconGuides on essential outdoor skills and subjects and field identification. The following titles are currently available, but this list grows every year. For a free catalog with a complete list of titles, call The Globe Pequot Press toll-free at 1-800-243-0495.

MOUNTAIN BIKING

Mountain Biking Arizona
Mountain Biking Colorado
Mountain Biking Georgia
Mountain Biking Idaho
Mountain Bikers Guide to New Mexico
Mountain Biking New York
Mountain Biking North Carolina
Mountain Biking Northern
New England
Mountain Biking Oregon
Mountain Biking Pennsylvania
Mountain Biking North Carolina
Mountain Biking South Carolina
Mountain Biking Southern California
Mountain Biking Southern
New England
Mountain Biking Utah
Mountain Biking Washington
Mountain Biking Wisconsin
Mountain Biking Wyoming

LOCAL CYCLING SERIES

Mountain Biking Albuquerque
Mountain Biking Bend
Mountain Biking Boise
Mountain Biking Bozeman
Mountain Biking Chequamegon
Mountain Biking Chico
Mountain Biking Colorado Springs
Mountain Biking Denver/Boulder
Mountain Biking Durango
Mountain Biking Flagstaff and
Sedona
Mountain Biking Helena
Mountain Biking Moab
Mountain Biking Spokane
Mountain Biking the Twin Cities
Mountain Biking Utah's St. George/
Cedar City Area
Mountain Biking White Mountains

■ *To order any of these books, check with your local*
bookseller or call The Globe Pequot Press at
1-800-243-0495
www.FalconGuide.com

FALCON®

FALCONGUIDES® Leading the Way™

www.Falcon.com

Since 1979, Falcon® has brought you the best in outdoor recreational guidebooks. Now you can access that same reliable and accurate information online.

❏ In-depth content, maps, and advice on a variety of outdoor activities, including hiking, climbing, biking, scenic driving, and wildlife viewing.

❏ A free monthly E-newsletter that delivers the latest news right to your inbox.

❏ Our popular games section where you can win prizes just by playing.

❏ An exciting and educational kids' section featuring online quizzes, coloring pages, and other activities.

❏ Outdoor forums where you can exchange ideas and tips with other outdoor enthusiasts.

❏ Also Falcon screensavers, online classified ads, and panoramic photos of spectacular destinations.

And much more!

*Plan your next outdoor adventure at
our web site. Point your browser to
www.FalconGuide.com and get FalconGuided!*